F

Laurie Blum's

FREE MONEY

for
Diseases
of Aging

A Fireside Book
Published by Simon & Schuster
New York   London   Toronto   Sydney   Tokyo   Singapore

FIRESIDE
Simon & Schuster Building
Rockefeller Center
1230 Avenue of the Americas
New York, New York 10020

Designed by Christina M. Riley
Manufactured in the United States of America

1 3 5 7 9 10 8 6 4 2

Library of Congress Cataloging-in-Publication Data
is available

ISBN 0-671-74592-1

· ·

I would like to briefly but sincerely thank my "A Team," Christina Riley, Deborah Brody, Tony Stanford, and Fori Kay, as well as my wonderful editor Ed Walters, and of course Alan Kellock.

Contents

Foreword

• •

by Michael E. Makover, M.D.
Assistant Professor of Clinical Medicine,
The New York University School of Medicine

In the "good old days," when the doctor made house calls, he carried all he could do for you in a little black bag. He sat by your side and you either got better or faded away. Today, modern medicine can do much more. Unfortunately, the technologies used in comprehensive medical treatment are very expensive. As a result, health care costs have skyrocketed. Added to the costs associated with technological advances are the costs of hospital, nursing and long-term care, which are further increased by a growing demand from an aging population. All Americans, except the most wealthy, face an immediate threat. Even the most careful, hard-working individual can suddenly find himself/herself overwhelmed by medical expenses resulting from a catastrophic illness. The best insurance policy may not be adequate to cover prolonged intensive care or long-term nursing care. Most insurance coverage now available is even more limited.

When my patients are financially strapped, I (like many other physicians) help by reducing or even eliminating my personal fees. But that is a drop in the bucket compared to the other costs the patient faces (e.g., hospitalization, laboratory tests, etc.). As a physician, I find it very painful to have to decide what care a patient receives based not on his physical condition but on the state of his wallet. Although arrangements can sometimes be made for hospitalization, tests or procedures, often the patient has to do without or settle for an inferior alternative.

You, the reader, must consider the possibility that you could be suddenly overwhelmed by medical costs. Health insurance is now so expensive that you may not be able to afford all that you need. Even with good coverage, health insurance cannot guarantee protection against all costs. Following acute care, you may require home nursing care or residence in a long-term care facility — either at a significant cost. Most people have little or no coverage for such expenses. Losing all one owns is not uncommon for the individual with a chronic illness.

Laurie Blum has provided you with an invaluable guide to resources you can use if serious or long-term illness — particularly if associated with aging — strikes you or someone in your family. Sometimes a hospital social worker can help you locate additional funds. Ms. Blum has gone beyond traditional resources to find funding sources often overlooked by social workers yet easy for you to use. Her extensive experience in fund-raising has given her insight into obtaining money from many disparate and obscure sources.

The best protection against high medical costs is, of course, prevention. Your lifestyle really matters. Nutrition, exercise, smoking, alcohol, drugs, and stress are not the boring subjects of school lectures. How you feel now and in the future depends almost entirely on what you do with the body you were given at birth. You can make a great difference for yourself with only modest effort. As I practice medicine, I find as much satisfaction in keeping my patients fit as I do in curing their ills.

Unfortunately, we cannot prevent everything, so it is best to be prepared. Get the best insurance coverage you can. Avoid HMOs and managed care, if possible, because these systems operate by rationing care and limiting your doctor's freedom to give you all that is available. Try to keep a reserve fund. Disability insurance is important, but you must calculate how much you need to live on, including the increased cost of being disabled.

Lastly, study Laurie Blum's book and be prepared to tap into all the free money you can. Your future may depend on it.

Introduction

. . . .

When a middle-class elderly person suffers a debilitating illness, such as Alzheimer's disease, that requires long-term custodial care, it can be devastating to a family, financially as well as emotionally. The poor are provided for by Medicaid. The rich have ample resources. But all too often those in the middle class see their life savings siphoned off until they, too, are poor and qualify for Medicaid. Elderly individuals on Medicare are liable for deductibles, coinsurance payments, and the costs of catastrophic illness that exceed Medicare's tight limits on hospital and physician reimbursements.

Older Americans will be especially prone to the rising costs of medical care in the 1990s. Medicare coverage is certain to be cut back over the next few years. Even now, Medicare does not cover care for Alzheimer's disease and many other long-term illnesses. As Medicare increasingly squeezes the medical community with cost caps and red tape, more and more doctors and hospitals will shun Medicare patients, as many already avoid those covered by Medicaid. Nursing home costs will pass the fifty billion dollar mark this year, and more than half of this amount is borne by patients and their families. Many corporations have made or are contemplating deep cuts in retirement health plans. These developments and others adversely affect the very people who are the biggest consumers of high-ticket health care.

Free Money for Diseases of Aging directs readers to the billions of dollars available annually not only for medical expenses but also for living expenses and long-term custodial care. Much of the available money is awarded without regard to the financial status of the recipient, and *none* of it ever needs to be paid back. The book includes information on funding available in all fifty states.

The book is divided into six chapters:

1) **"Associations: Funding and Referral Information"** (listing foundations and associations that provide a wide range of services, including: supplying information on the disease; sponsoring and referring patients and their families to support groups; and providing physician referrals, funds for research, and patient services);

2) **"Private Foundation Funding"** (listing possible sources both for monies for direct medical expenses such as doctor and hospital bills, and for reimbursement for the loss of regular income that is often a devastating side-effect of illness);

3) **"Corporate/Employee Grants"** (listing companies and corporations that provide grants for their employees or former employees);

4) **"Flow-through Funding"** (providing information about foundation monies that are given to individuals through sponsoring nonprofit organizations);

5) **"State and Regional Government Grants"** (including local state health care offices, as well as native health service grants, which provide funds for American Indians and Native Alaskans); and

6) **"Federal Grants"** (identifying agencies offering direct funding and/or essential referral information).

Where possible, listings within each chapter are arranged state-by-state to make this book as easy to use as possible. Check your state's listings in all six chapters to see which grants or corporate programs apply to you. You'll find funding parameters and an address and phone number to contact for further information (and application forms).

By the time this book is published, some of the information contained here will have changed. No reference book can be as up-to-date as the reader or the author would like. Names, addresses, dollar amounts, telephone numbers, and other data are always in flux; however, most of the information will not have changed.

While reviewing this data, readers are advised to remember that funding sources are not without restrictions and that researching, applying for, and receiving aid will take time, effort, diligence, and thought. You are going to have to identify the sources of aid for which you qualify and determine whether or not you fulfill geographic and other requirements. You are going to have to fill out applications. You may meet with rejection and frustration somewhere along this road. The odds, however, are in your favor that you will qualify for some sort of funding assistance.

On the next pages is a concise, how-to guide to writing a grant proposal. Follow my instructions and you should be successful in obtaining some sort of assistance. Good luck.

How to apply

. . . .

As indicated by the number of listings in this book, thousands of resources for health-related funding exist throughout the country from government, private foundation, and corporate sources. Applying for this aid is the challenging part; it requires diligence, thought and organization.

First is the sorting out or research/gathering phase. Look through each chapter of the book and mark each potential assistance source. Pay close attention to the listed restrictions and qualifications, eliminating from your list the resources least likely to assist you.

Then, politely contact each of your listed sources by mail or phone to verify all current information, such as address, telephone, name of the proper contact, and his/her title (in cases where the contact's name is not listed, begin your letter, "To Whom It May Concern"). At this time, you can also arrange to get a copy of the source's most current assistance guidelines, and an application form if one is required. Use this opportunity to find out about any application deadlines and to ask where you are in the funding cycle (i.e., if there is no deadline, when would be the best time to apply; also, be sure to ask when awards will be announced and funds distributed). However, do not "grill" or cross-examine the person you reach on the phone. Always be prepared to talk about why you are applying and what you are applying for — in case you ring through to the key decisionmaker, who decides to interview you on the spot!

Second is the application phase. Most often you will be asked to submit a formal application (rather than a proposal). Always be sure to read (and follow!) the instructions for completing the application. Usually the same material used for one application can be applied to most, if not all, of your other applications, with a little restructuring to make sure you answer each and every question as asked, appropriate to each application.

Grant applications take time (and thought) to fill out, so make sure you give yourself enough time to thoroughly complete the application before its deadline. Filling out the application can be a lengthy process, because you may be required to write one or more essays. Often, what is required is a "statement of purpose" explaining what you will use the money for and sometimes explaining why you need the assistance for which you are applying. You may also need time to assemble required attachments, such as tax returns and other financial records. (Don't worry, in most cases, you won't be penalized for having money in the bank.) You may also be required to include personal references. Be sure to get strong references. Call all of the people you plan to list, and ask them if they feel comfortable giving you references. Remember, you have to convince the grantors to give money to you and not to someone else.

Be clear, concise and neat! You may very well prepare a top-notch application, but it won't look good if it's been prepared in a sloppy manner. Applications (and proposals) should always be typed and double-spaced. Make sure you keep a copy after you send off the original — I have learned the hard way that there is nothing worse than having the funding source be unable to find your application and your having to reconstruct it because you didn't keep a copy.

You should apply to a number of funding sources for grants and awards, as no one application is guaranteed to win an award. Although none of the sources listed in this book requires an application fee, the effort you will have to put in will probably limit you to a maximum of eight applications (if you are ambitious and want to apply to more than eight sources, go right ahead). Remember, the more sources you apply to, the greater your chances for success.

COMPONENTS OF
A SUCCESSFUL PROPOSAL

One of the largest categories of grants that are given to individuals are grants for general welfare and medical assistance, that is "free money" for emergency or long-term personal, medical, or living expenses. The various funding agencies that make these awards have happily made applying for these grants much simpler than for other categories. Most, if not all, of the foundations you will be applying to will require the following in order to consider your request for funding:

1. A brief but concise letter outlining you or your family member's medical problem and/or expenses and bills you have incurred because of this problem. In the final paragraph of your letter you should specify a dollar amount that you feel confident would ease your financial burden (i.e., "I request a grant in the amount of $2,500 to help me pay the costs associated with a visiting nurse which is not covered by my medical insurance."). Remember to carefully look at the money given in the foundation listing you are applying to; If the foundation only gives grants ranging from $5,000 to $15,000 and you need $20,000, you can only request that which the foundation gives.

2. A report from the doctors or hospital staff involved with the patient on whose behalf the grant is being submitted. Because of the enormous volume of mail that most foundations receive, you may want to get the medical reports directly from doctors and/or hospital personnel and submit them with your application. This way there is no chance that a foundation can delay or turn down your application on the grounds that it is incomplete.

3. A copy of your tax return. Do not panic! You will not be penalized for showing excellent earnings or having savings. The issue is how the costs associated with the medical problems or care needs that you are faced with alter your financial stability. However, if you are in financial need you will certainly be given every consideration.

4. A personal interview. This may take place by phone or in person. Stay calm. Foundations are run by people committed to their mission of helping those in need or in trouble. Simply state the facts of your case and needs and all will go well.

Remember, your application should be clear and concise. Your letter should not exceed two pages. Be sure to include any attachments the foundation might require such as medical reports and tax returns. Follow my instructions and you should qualify for some sort of "free money."

Associations:
Funding and
Referral Information

• • • • • • • • • • • • • • • • • • •

This chapter is an invaluable resource guide for the patient and his/her family. It contains listings of foundations/associations that address the needs of individuals with specific diseases. Among the many services they provide, these organizations publish information about the disease, sponsor and refer patients and their families to support groups, give physician referrals, and award funds for research as well as for patient services. Though not all of the foundations/associations offer monies to be paid directly to patients, I felt it was imperative that I include this information in this book. Having experienced catastrophic illness firsthand, I know all too well the comfort and support that a professional association offers the patient and his/her family, who are frightened and overwhelmed.

The chapter is organized alphabetically, by name of disease. The various associations/foundations are listed alphabetically under the names of the diseases they address.

Patients and their families will probably find, as I have, that the various staff members of these foundations/associations are exceedingly helpful during difficult times. Use them and their associations to your best advantage.

ASSOCIATIONS

. . . .

American Association for Continuity of Care
720 Light Street
Baltimore, MD 21230
(301) 837-1600

Description: Association of health care professionals involved in discharge planning, social work, hospital administration, home care, long-term care, home health agencies, and continuity of care
Contact: Carol T. Shaner, Executive Director

American Association of Kidney Patients
1 Davis Blvd.
Suite LL1
Tampa, FL 33606
(813) 251-0725

Description: Membership open to persons on hemodialysis, peritoneal dialysis, and kidney transplants as well as to their families and friends and to professionals in the dialysis field; provides educational services to patients and public about kidney disease, and works to improve quality of care for all patients; promotes kidney donor programs
Contact: Richard B. Baumann, Executive Director

American Federation of Home Health Agencies
1320 Fenwick Lane
Suite 100
Silver Spring, MD 20910
(301) 588-1454

Description: Federation of agencies providing home therapeutic services such as nursing, speech therapy, and physical therapy
Contact: Ann Howard, Executive Director

The American Kidney Fund
6110 Executive Blvd.
Suite 1010
Rockville, MD 20852
(301) 881-3052
(800) 638-8299

Description: Seeks to alleviate the financial burdens caused by kidney disease and to improve the quality of life for kidney patients; supports dialysis center emergency funds
Contact: Francis J. Soldovere, Executive Director

• • • • • • • • • • • • • • • • • • •

**American Liver
Foundation**
1425 Pompton Avenue
Cedar Grove, NJ 07009
(201) 256-2550
(800) 223-0179

Description: Distributes information on liver diseases, liver functions and preventive measures; sponsors support groups for liver disease patients and their families; provides physician referral service
Contact: Thelma King Thiel, President

**American Lung
Association**
1740 Broadway
New York, NY 10019
(212) 315-8700

Description: A federation of state and local associations of physicians, nurses, and laypersons concerned about the prevention and control of lung disease; coordinates with other organizations in planning and conducting programs in community services, public, professional and patient education, and research
Contact: John R. Garrison, Managing Director

**American Society of
Nephrology**
1101 Connecticut Avenue
NW
Suite 700
Washington, DC 20036
(202) 857-1190

Description: Contributes to the education of nephrologists and seeks to improve the quality of patient care
Contact: Judith Walker, Executive Director

**American Hospital
Association**
Division of Ambulatory
Care and Health Promotion
840 N. Lake Shore Drive
Chicago, IL 60611
(312) 280-6461

Description: Supports hospitals and other health care providers with interests in ambulatory care, emergency services, home care, health maintenance organizations, and hospices
Contact: Diane M. Howard, Director

ASSOCIATIONS

• • • • • • • • • • • • • • • • • • •

Emphysema Anonymous, Inc.
P.O. Box 3224
Seminole, FL 34642
(813) 391-9977

Description: Aids victims of emphysema through education, encouragement, and mutual assistance. National office provides nonmedical counseling service for patients and their families
Contact: William E. Jaeckle, Executive Director

National Association for Ventilator Dependent Individuals
3607 Poplar Street
P.O. Box 3666
Erie, PA 16508
(814) 455-6171

Description: A support group for individuals requiring short or long term use of ventilators due to respiratory ailments; distributes information related to ventilator-dependency services, resources, and education
Contact: Daniel W. Dubowski, President

National Kidney Foundation
30 East 33rd Street
Suite 1100
New York, NY 10016
(212) 889-2210
(800) 622-9010

Description: Supports research, patient services, professional and public education, organ donor programs, and community service; affiliates conduct community and patient services (drug banks, transportation, early screening, patient seminars, etc.)
Contact: John Davis, Executive Director

National Kidney and Urologic Diseases Information Clearinghouse
P.O. Box NKUDIC
9000 Rockville Pike
Bethseda, MD 20892
(301) 468-6345

Description: A networking, referral, and resource service; distributes educational information on kidney and urologic diseases and their causes and treatments and provides direct responses to written and telephone inquiries
Contact: Elizabeth H. Singer, Director

North American Society for Dialysis and Transplantation
c/o Dr. Wadi Suke
6550 Fannin, Suite 500
Houston, TX 77030
(713) 790-3275

Description: Association of nephrologists, transplant surgeons and physicians, and allied health professionals; promotes education and research and distributes information on current knowledge and technology in the field of kidney dialysis and transplantation
Contact: Dr. Wadi Suki, Secretary-Treasurer

United Ostomy Association
36 Executive Park
Suite 120
Irvine, CA 92714
(714) 660-8624

Description: Open to persons who have lost the normal function of their bowel or bladder necessitating colostomy, ileostomy, ileal conduit, or ureterostomy surgery (known collectively as ostomy); supports the rehabilitation of these individuals through mutual aid, moral support, and exchange of practical information in managing the stoma and its necessary prosthetic appliances
Contact: Darlene Smith, Executive Director

Private Foundation Funding

The listings in this chapter are probably the easiest and most accessible funding sources for the average individual seeking a grant. Until now, this information has not been readily available to the general public. And yet thousands of foundations give away millions of dollars to individuals to help them pay for medical treatment for major, long-term and chronic illnesses. In many cases, foundations also provide funding to help individuals cope with the loss of regular income that is often a devastating side-effect of such illnesses.

Do you just walk up, hold out your hand, and expect someone to put money in it? Of course not. Getting grant money takes time, effort, and thought on your part. You are going to have to find out who is giving away money. You are going to have to fill out applications. You may meet with frustration or rejection somewhere down the road. The odds, however, are in your favor that you will qualify for some sort of funding.

The information in this chapter is organized by state. Wherever possible, each listing includes a description of what the foundation funds, any restrictions (i.e., you must reside in a particular town or city), the total amount of money awarded annually, the number of grants or loans made annually, the range of monies given, the average size of the award, information on how to apply, deadline date(s), and name(s) of contact person(s).

PRIVATE FOUNDATION FUNDING

. . . .

ALABAMA

Kate Kinloch Middleton Fund
P.O. Drawer 2527
Mobile, AL 36601
phone: N/A

Description: Grants or low-interest loans to help defray the costs of unexpected serious illness
Restrictions: Limited to residents of Mobile County, Alabama
$ Given: In FY89, 63 grants totaling $108,286 were awarded to individuals; range, $135 - $8,094.
Application Information: Initial approach by interview
Deadline: N/A
Contact: Joan Sapp

CALIFORNIA

William Babcock Memorial Endowment
305 San Anselmo Ave.
Suite 219
San Anselmo, CA 94960
(415) 453-0901

Description: Grants or loans to persons burdened with exceptional medical expenses which exceed insurance coverage and fall outside the purview of other community agencies
Restrictions: Limited to persons who have been residents of Marin County, California, for two or more years
$ Given: In FY89, 480 grants totaling $445,170 were awarded to individuals; range, $50 - $10,000.
Application Information: Call for application guidelines; formal application required.
Deadline: None
Contact: Executive Director

Albert B. Cutter Memorial Fund
Security Pacific National Bank
Trust Department
P.O. Box 712
Riverside, CA 92502
(714) 781-1523

ADDITIONAL ADDRESS:
P.O. Box 3189, Terminal Annex, Los Angeles, CA 92501

Description: Limited grants to persons in extreme circumstances who are not eligible for other sources of aid
Restrictions: Applicants must have been permanent residents of Riverside, California for at least one year, and must have been referred by a local agency.
$ Given: In 1989, 26 grants totaling $6,650 were awarded to individuals; range, $22 - $550.
Application Information: Applications are accepted from local agencies; individuals are referred by these agencies; formal application required; interview or presentation required.
Deadline: None
Contact: Executive Secretary, Trust Department

Jefferson (John Percival and Mary C.) Endowment Fund
114 East De La Guerra
Santa Barbara, CA 93102
(805) 963-8822

Description: Emergency relief assistance for medical, dental and living expenses
Restrictions: Limited to residents of Santa Barbara County, California
$ Given: In FY89, 30 grants totaling $63,000 were awarded to individuals; range, $100-$6,500.
Application Information: Initial contact by letter; formal application required
Deadline: N/A
Contact: Patricia M. Brouard, Trustee

Virginia Scatena Memorial Fund for San Francisco School Teachers
c/o Bank of America, N.A.
555 California Street
17th Floor
San Francisco, CA 94104
phone: N/A

Description: Financial assistance to retired San Francisco school teachers who are needy, sick, or disabled.
Restrictions: Limited to retired teachers of the San Francisco Public School Department
$ Given: Total grants range from $125 - $400.
Application Information: Formal application required
Deadline: None; applications reviewed semi-annually by advisory committee
Contact: Susan Morales

PRIVATE FOUNDATION FUNDING

Sequoia Trust Fund
555 California Street
36th Floor
San Francisco, CA 94104
(415) 393-8552

Description: Financial assistance to "needy people who, by their special talents, have given great pleasure to others."
Restrictions: Assistance for special or unusual medical expenses; primarily for California residents
$ Given: In FY89, two grants totaling $4,400 were awarded to individuals; range, $2,000 - $2,400.
Application Information: Initial contact by letter; formal application required
Deadline: None
Contact: Walter M. Baird, Secretary

CONNECTICUT

**Blue Horizon Health &
Welfare Trust**
c/o Reid & Riege
Lakeville, CT 06039
(203) 435-9894

Description: Financial assistance for medical costs.
Restrictions: Limited to residents of Connecticut
$ Given: Grant awards range from $25 - $543
Application Information: Initial contact by letter
Deadline: None
Contact: Frances M. Wagner, Trustee

Marion Isabelle Coe Fund
c/o Colonial Bank and
Trust Company
P.O. Box 2210
Waterbury, CT 06722
phone: N/A

Description: Relief assistance to adults for living and medical expenses. Grants provide continuing assistance to needy individuals, enabling them to remain in their own homes. Awards paid in monthly installments, and are renewed annually.
Restrictions: Limited to residents of Goshen, Litchfield, Morris, and Warren, Connecticut
$ Given: Monthly awards range from $45 to $140; average, $100
Application Information: Initial contact by letter
Deadline: None
Contact: Mrs. Speers

• • • • • • • • • • • • • • • • • • •

James Crocker
Testamentary Trust
P.O. Box 1045
Canaan, CT 06018
phone: N/A

Description: Temporary assistance to individuals in extreme financial difficulty
Restrictions: Limited to residents of Winchester, Connecticut
$ Given: Grants range from $11 - $500.
Application Information: Most applications are unsolicited and not preselected. Applicants are typically referred to the Funds Manager by local clergy of all denominations. Information concerning immediate financial need required.
Deadline: N/A
Contact: Kevin F. Nelligan

The de Kay Foundation
c/o Manufacturers Hanover
Trust Company
270 Park Avenue
New York, NY 10017
(212) 270-6000

Description: Grants to elderly individuals in financial need, particularly to those who are sick or disabled or who lack proper care.
Restrictions: Limited to residents of New York, New Jersey, and Connecticut
$ Given: In FY89, 83 grants totaling $202,540 were awarded to individuals; range, $350 - $7,150; general range, $1,000 - $5, 000
Application Information: Initial approach by letter; formal application required
Deadline: None
Contact: Lloyd Saltus II, Vice President

St. Luke's Nurses
Benefit Fund
47 Phillips Lane
Darien, CT 06820
phone: N/A

Description: Grants for needy graduates of St. Luke's School of Nursing.
Restrictions: Limited to St. Luke's alumnae
$ Given: In FY89, one grant for $2,000 was awarded
Application Information: Formal application required
Deadline: None
Contact: Martha Kirk, Trustee

PRIVATE FOUNDATION FUNDING

. . . .

The Westport-Weston Foundation
c/o The Westport Bank & Trust Company
P.O. Box 5177
Westport, CT 06881
(203) 222-6911

Description: Grants for medical and basic living expenses
Restrictions: Limited to residents of Westport and Weston, Connecticut
$ Given: Grants range from $50 - $400.
Application Information: Initial contact by letter
Deadline: N/A
Contact: Susanne M. Allen, Trust Officer

Widow's Society
20 Bayberry Lane
Avon, CT 06001
(203) 678-9660

Description: Financial assistance to needy women
Restrictions: Limited to residents of Connecticut
$ Given: In FY89, 118 grants totaling $122,824 were awarded to individuals; range, $75 - $4,800.
Application Information: Applications are typically referred through social service agencies, but individuals may also submit letters.
Deadline: N/A
Contact: Dorothy Johnson, President

DELAWARE

Delaware Foundation - Quigly Trust
P.O. Box 1669
Wilmington, DE 19899
phone: N/A

Description: Grants for medication and medical care
Restrictions: Limited to residents of Delaware
$ Given: Grants range from $50 - $1,500.
Application Information: Formal application required; request application form from the foundation
Deadline: None
Contact: N/A

• • • • • • • • • • • • • • • • • • • •

FLORIDA

Gore Family Memorial Foundation
501 East Las Olas
Fort Lauderdale, FL 33302
phone: N/A

Description: One-time and short-term assistance grants for medical expenses, equipment for the handicapped, and housing and transportation costs
Restrictions: Limited to residents of Broward County, Florida, and surrounding areas
$ Given: In FY89, 390 relief assistance grants totaling $279,250 were awarded to individuals.
Application Information: Write for application guidelines
Deadline: None
Contact: N/A

Roy M. Speer Foundation
1803 U.S. Highway 19
Holiday, FL 34691-5536
phone: N/A

Description: Grants to individuals in financial difficulty as a result of medical problems
Restrictions: Limited to residents of Florida
$ Given: One grant for $4,000 is awarded.
Application Information: Initial approach by letter
Deadline: None
Contact: N/A

Winter Haven Hospital Charity Fund
c/o NCNB National Bank
P.O. Box 199
Orlando, FL 32802
phone: N/A

Description: Grants for medical assistance to the financially distressed
Restrictions: Limited to residents of Winter Haven, Florida
$ Given: In FY89, two grants were awarded to individuals; range, $250 - $1,500.
Application Information: Write for guidelines
Deadline: None
Contact: N/A

PRIVATE FOUNDATION FUNDING

. . . .

GEORGIA

Baker (Clark and Ruby) Foundation
c/o Bank South
Personal Trust Department
P.O. Box 4956 (MC45)
Atlanta, GA 30302-8924
(404) 529-4627

Description: Grants primarily to retired Methodist ministers for pensions and medical assistance
Restrictions: Residents of Georgia
$ Given: 10 grants totaling $15,500 are awarded to individuals.
Application Information: Initial approach by letter or phone; interviews required
Deadline: None
Contact: Richard L. Watton, Trust Officer

Thomas C. Burke Foundation
182 Riley Avenue
No. B
Macon, GA 31204-2345
(912) 745-1442

Description: Medical assistance in one of three forms: (1) one-time payments for doctor bills, medical equipment and pharmacy bills; (2) weekly grants of up to $60 to assist with medical expenses; or (3) grants for transportation to medical facilities
Restrictions: Limited to residents of Bibb County, Georgia
$ Given: In FY89, an unspecified number of grants totaling $120,772 were awarded to individuals.
Application Information: Initial contact by phone
Deadline: None
Contact: Carolyn P. Griggers

Pine Mountain Benevolent Foundation, Inc.
P.O. Box 2301
Columbus, GA 31902
phone: N/A

Description: Welfare assistance to individuals living in Georgia
Restrictions: Limited to residents of Georgia
$ Given: In FY89, two grants totaling $2,200 were awarded to individuals; range, $500 - $1,500.
Application Information: Write for guidelines
Deadline: None
Contact: Cason J. Callaway, Jr.

. . . .

HAWAII

The Hawaii Community Foundation
222 Merchant Street
Honolulu, HI 96813
(808) 537-6333

Program: Winifred D. Robertson Fund
Description: One-time assistance to adult residents of Oahu, Hawaii

Program: Alice M.G. Soper Fund
Description: One-time grants to adults, age 50 or older in financial need due to illness or disability

Program: Gwenfried Allen Fund
Description: Financial assistance for the elderly and mentally ill

Restrictions (for all programs): Limited to residents of Hawaii
$ Given: In 1989, 116 grants totaling $78,111 were awarded to individuals; range, $80 - $1,500; general range, $100 - $1,000; average, $680.
Application Information: Call for application guidelines; formal application required
Deadline: None
Contact: Suzanne Toguchi, Program Officer

ILLINOIS

Reade Industrial Fund
c/o Harris Trust and Savings Bank
P.O. Box 755
111 West Monroe Street
Chicago, IL 60690
(312) 461-7550

Description: Loans or grants to individuals who — through accidental injury, illness of themselves or family members, or inability to work — are unable to care for themselves, their spouses and their children
Restrictions: Limited to individuals who are currently or who have previously been employed in industry in Illinois
$ Given: Grants range from $373 - $5,000.
Application Information: Initial approach by letter; formal application required
Deadline: None
Contact: Tony Abiera

PRIVATE FOUNDATION FUNDING

• •

Swiss Benevolent Society of Chicago
P.O. Box 2137
Chicago, IL 60690
phone: N/A

Description: Grants to elderly and other individuals of Swiss descent or nationality in cases of need or emergency
Restrictions: Limited to Chicago area residents of Swiss descent or nationality
$ Given: 55 grants totaling $53,450 are awarded to individuals.
Application Information: Formal application required; write for program information and current program deadlines
Deadline: Varies
Contact: Admiral Alan Weber, President

KANSAS

Charlotte Hill Charitable Trust
P.O. Box 754
Winfield, KS 67156
(316) 221-4600

Description: Grants to single women over age 60 with limited income and assets
Restrictions: Limited to residents of the Arkansas City and Winfield, Kansas, areas
$ Given: In FY89, 62 grants totaling $75,700 were awarded to individuals; range, $40 - $5,900.
Application Information: Formal application required
Deadline: None
Contact: Loyette Olson

MAINE

Camden Home for Senior Citizens
66 Washington Street
Camden, ME 04843
(207) 236-2087
APPLICATION ADDRESS:
Belfast Road, Camden, ME 04843, (207) 236-2014

Description: Grants for such needs as medical care and drugs
Restrictions: Limited to residents of Camden, Rockport, Lincolnville, and Hope, Maine
$ Given: In FY89, 201 grants totaling $42,350 were awarded to individuals; range, $50 - $300.
Application Information: Write or call for guidelines
Deadline: None
Contact: Charles Lowe, President

Anita Card Montgomery Foundation
20 Mechanic Street
Camden, ME 04843-1707
phone: N/A

Description: Financial assistance for needy individuals, including funding for medical and dental expenses
Restrictions: Limited to residents of Camden, Rockport, Lincolnville, and Hope, Maine
$ Given: Grants range from $40 - $4,058.
Application Information: Write for guidelines
Deadline: None
Contact: Robert C. Perkins

Portland Female Charitable Society
c/o Janet Matty
20 Noyes Street
Portland, ME 04103
phone: N/A
APPLICATION ADDRESS:
142 Pleasant Street, No. 761, Portland, ME 04101

Description: Financial aid for such needs as health care, food and shelter. Emphasis on the needs of children, the aged, and the sick
Restrictions: Strictly limited to residents of Portland, Maine
$ Given: In FY89, 33 grants totaling $9,550 were awarded to individuals; range, $20 - $850.
Application Information: Full information required; applications usually presented by social workers, health care professionals, etc.; interviews required
Deadline: None
Contact: Janet Matty

Herbert E. Wadsworth Trust
c/o Fleet Bank of Maine
Merrill Center
Exchange Street
Bangor, ME 04401
phone: N/A

Description: Financial assistance for citizens of Winthrop, Maine, who are hospitalized in a well-regulated and recognized facility outside the town of Winthrop
Restrictions: Limited to citizens of Winthrop, Maine
$ Given: In FY89, nine grants totaling $8,440 were awarded to individuals; range, $100 - $3,150.
Application Information: Write for guidelines
Deadline: None
Contact: N/A

PRIVATE FOUNDATION FUNDING

MARYLAND

Anna Emory Warfield Memorial Fund, Inc.
103 West Monument Street
Baltimore, MD 21201
(301) 547-0612

Description: Relief assistance to elderly women in the Baltimore, Maryland, area
Restrictions: Limited to women in the Baltimore, Maryland, area
$ Given: In 1989, 42 grants totaling $150,000 were awarded to individuals; range, $900 - $3,925.
Application Information: Write to request application guidelines; formal application required
Deadline: None
Contact: Thelma K. O'Neal, Secretary

MASSACHUSETTS

The Pilgrim Foundation
478 Torrey Street
Brockton, MA 02401-4654
(508) 586-6100

Description: Financial assistance to families and children
Restrictions: Limited to residents of Brockton, Massachusetts
$ Given: Welfare assistance grants totaling $7,230 are awarded to individuals.
Application Information: Formal application required
Deadline: N/A
Contact: Executive Director

Charlotte M. Robbins Trust
c/o State Street Bank & Trust Company
P.O. Box 351
Boston, MA 02101
(617) 654-3360
APPLICATION ADDRESS:
c/o State Street Bank, 225 Franklin Street, Boston, MA 02110

Description: Financial assistance to aged couples and aged women
Restrictions: Limited to aged residents of the towns of Groton, Ayer, Harvard, Shirley, and Littleton, Massachusetts
$ Given: In 1989, total giving was $6,000.
Application Information: Write letter to application address, stating income, expenses, assets, and reason money is needed
Deadline: N/A
Contact: Cheryl D. Curtin, Vice President

• • • • • • • • • • • • • • • • • • • •

Salem Female Charitable Society
175 Federal Street
Boston, MA 02110
phone: N/A
APPLICATION ADDRESS:
30 Chestnut Street, Salem, MA 01970

Description: Financial aid to needy women of the Salem, Massachusetts, area
Restrictions: Original grant limited to residents of the Salem, Massachusetts, area; recipients may, however, relocate without forfeiting grant.
$ Given: In FY89, 18 grants totaling $19,810 were awarded to individuals; range, $200 - $1,700; average, $800
Application Information: Write for guidelines
Deadline: None
Contact: Jane A. Phillips, Treasurer

Shaw Fund for Mariners' Children
c/o Russell Brier & Co.
50 Congress Street
Room 800
Boston, MA 02109
phone: N/A
APPLICATION ADDRESS:
64 Concord Avenue, Norwood, MA 02062

Description: Grants to financially distressed mariners and their families
Restrictions: Limited to mariners, their wives or widows, and their children; Massachusetts residents only
$ Given: Grants totaling $114,140 are awarded to individuals.
Application Information: Write for program information
Deadline: None
Contact: Clare M. Tolias

The Swasey Fund for Relief of Public School Teachers of Newburyport, Inc.
31 Milk Street
Boston, MA 02109
(508) 462-2784
APPLICATION ADDRESS:
23 Summit Place, Newburyport, MA 01950

Description: Financial aid to individuals who have taught in the Newburyport, Massachusetts public school system for at least 10 years
Restrictions: See above
$ Given: In FY89, 21 grants totaling $66,600 were awarded to individuals; range, $100 - $10,000.
Application Information: Formal application required
Deadline: None
Contact: Jean MacDonald, Treasurer

PRIVATE FOUNDATION FUNDING

• • • • • • • • • • • • • • • • • • •

Urann Foundation
P.O. Box 1788
Brockton, MA 02403
(508) 588-7744

Description: Medical assistance grants for Massachusetts families engaged in cranberry farming and processing. Grants intended to assist in payment of hospital and medical bills
Restrictions: Limited to families located in Massachusetts
$ Given: In 1989, 22 grants totaling $44,460 were awarded to individuals; 1 medical assistance grant for $680 was awarded.
Application Information: Initial contact by phone or letter
Deadline: None
Contact: Howard Whelan, Administrator

MINNESOTA

Hanna R. Kristianson Trust
P.O. Box 1011
Albert Lea, MN 56007
APPLICATION ADDRESS:
Clarks Grove, MN 56016
(507) 256-4415

Description: Financial aid to needy individuals over 50 years of age
Restrictions: Limited to residents of Freeborn County, Minnesota who are over 50 years old
$ Given: Grants range from $20 - $1,660.
Application Information: Call or write for guidelines
Deadline: None
Contact: Richard S. Haug, Trustee

Charles D. Gilfillan Paxton Memorial, Inc.
c/o Thomas W. Murray, Vice President
W-555 First National Bank Building
St. Paul, MN 55101
(612) 291-6236
APPLICATION ADDRESS:
Committee of Beneficiaries, 200 Southwest First Street, Rochester, MN 55905, (507) 282-2511

Description: Medical assistance to financially distressed Minnesota residents; priority given to those in areas and towns with populations of less than 3,000
Restrictions: Limited to residents of Minnesota
$ Given: In FY89, 80 grants totaling $39,900 were awarded to individuals; range, $38 - $2,16; average, $500.
Application Information: Formal application required
Deadline: None
Contact: Marie LaPlante, Secretary

• • • • • • • • • • • • • • • • • • • •

The Saint Paul Foundation
1120 Norwest Center
St. Paul, MN 55101
(612) 224-5463

Description: Relief assistance grants
Restrictions: Limited to residents of St. Paul and Minneapolis, Minnesota, and to employees of 3M Company
$ Given: 15 relief assistance grants totaling $42,504 are awarded to individuals.
Application Information: Write or call for guidelines
Deadline: N/A
Contact: Paul A. Verret, President

MISSOURI

Herschend Family Foundation
c/o Jack R. Herschend
Silver Dollar City, Inc.
Branson, MO 65616
(417) 338-2611

Description: Assistance for individuals in need
Restrictions: Intended primarily for residents of Missouri
$ Given: In 1989, 34 grants totaling $250,430 were awarded to individuals.
Application Information: Call or write, explaining need
Deadline: None
Contact: Jack R. Herschend, Director

NEW HAMPSHIRE

Abbie M. Griffin Hospital Fund
111 Concord Street
Nashua, NH 03060
phone: N/A

Description: Grants for payment of hospital bills
Restrictions: Limited to residents of Merrimack, Hillsborough County, New Hampshire
$ Given: Four grants totaling $11,000 are awarded to individuals; range, $2,221 - $3,370.
Application Information: Write for guidelines
Deadline: None
Contact: S. Robert Winer, Trustee

PRIVATE FOUNDATION FUNDING

NEW JERSEY

The de Kay Foundation
c/o Manufacturers Hanover
Trust Company
270 Park Avenue
New York, NY 10017
(212) 270-6000

Description: Grants to elderly individuals in financial need, particularly to those who are sick or disabled or who lack proper care
Restrictions: Limited to residents of New York, New Jersey, and Connecticut
$ Given: In FY89, 82 grants totaling $202,540 were awarded to individuals; range, $350 - $7,150; general range, $1,000 - $5, 000.
Application Information: Initial approach by letter; formal application required
Deadline: None
Contact: Lloyd Saltus II, Vice President

Otto Sussman Trust
P.O. Box 1374
Trainsmeadow Station
Flushing, NY 11370-9998
phone: N/A

Description: Financial assistance for medical bills and caregiving expenses to individuals with serious or terminal illnesses
Restrictions: Limited to residents of New York, New Jersey, Oklahoma, and Pennsylvania
$ Given: Grants range from $329 - $4,000.
Application Information: Write letter requesting application form and guidelines; explain circumstances of need; formal application required
Deadline: None
Contact: Edward S. Miller, Trustee

NEW YORK

The James Gordon Bennett Memorial Corporation
c/o New York Daily News
220 East 42nd Street
New York, NY 10017
phone: N/A

Description: Grants to journalists who have been employees of a daily New York City newspaper for ten years or more. Acceptance based on need. Funds to be used for "the physical needs of persons . . . who, by reason of old age, accident or bodily infirmity, or through lack of means, are unable to care for themselves."
Restrictions: Priority given to journalists who have worked in the borough of Manhattan.

• • • • • • • • • • • • • • • • • •

(continued)

$ Given: Grants range from $150 - $6,000.
Application Information: Write for guidelines and program information; formal application required
Deadline: None
Contact: Denise Houseman

Brockway Foundation for the Needy of the Village and Township of Homer, New York
c/o Key Bank
25 South Main Street
Homer, NY 13077-1314
phone: N/A

Description: Financial assistance based on need
Restrictions: Limited to residents of the Homer, New York, area
$ Given: Grants range from $180 - $600.
Application Information: Write for guidelines
Deadline: None
Contact: M. Lee Swartwout, Treasurer

The Clark Foundation
30 Wall Street
New York, NY 10005
(212) 269-1833

Description: Financial aid for medical and hospital care to needy individuals in upstate New York and New York City
Restrictions: Limited to residents of upstate New York and New York City
$ Given: In FY89, 18 grants totaling $108,327 were awarded to individuals; range, $560 - $15,600.
Application Information: Write for guidelines
Deadline: None
Contact: Edward W. Stack, Secretary

Josiah H. Danforth Memorial Fund
8 Fremont Street
Gloversville, NY 12078
phone: N/A

Description: Financial aid for medical care
Restrictions: Limited to residents of Fulton County, NY
$ Given: In 1989, 95 grants totaling $18,610 were awarded to individuals; range, $16 - $500; average, $200; maximum grant per year per person, $500.
Application Information: Write for guidelines, application form; formal application required
Deadline: None
Contact: N/A

PRIVATE FOUNDATION FUNDING

. . . .

The de Kay Foundation
c/o Manufacturers Hanover
Trust Company
270 Park Avenue
New York, NY 10017
(212) 270-6000

Description: Grants to elderly individuals in financial need, particularly to those who are sick or disabled or who lack proper care
Restrictions: Limited to residents of New York, New Jersey and Connecticut
$ Given: In FY89, 82 grants totaling $202,540 were awarded to individuals; range, $350 - $7,150; general range, $1,000 - $5, 000.
Application Information: Write to request application forms; formal application required
Deadline: None
Contact: Lloyd Saltus II, Vice President

Mary W. MacKinnon Fund
c/o Wilber National Bank
Trust Department
245 Main Street
Oneonta, NY 13820
phone: N/A

Description: Funding for medical, hospital, nursing home and rehabilitative care for elderly and indigent residents of Sidney, New York.
Restrictions: Limited to residents of Sidney, New York
$ Given: Grants totaling $48,453 are awarded to individuals.
Application Information: Applications must be submitted through a physician or hospital
Deadline: None
Contact: N/A

Saranac Lake Voluntary Health Association, Inc.
70 Main Street
Saranac Lake, NY 12983-1706
phone: N/A

Description: Provides funding for visiting nurse services for the elderly in Saranac Lake, New York, as well as grants for dental services to students
Restrictions: Limited to residents of Saranac Lake, New York
$ Given: In FY89, three grants totaling $42,120 were awarded to individuals; range, $4,498 - $31,613.
Application Information: Write for guidelines
Deadline: N/A
Contact: N/A

• • • • • • • • • • • • • • • • • • • •

St. Luke's Nurses Benefit Fund
47 Phillips Lane
Darien, CT 06820
phone: N/A

Description: Grants for needy graduates of St. Luke's School of Nursing
Restrictions: Limited to St. Luke's alumnae
$ Given: In FY89, one grant for $2,000 was awarded
Application Information: Formal application required
Deadline: None
Contact: Martha Kirk, Trustee

Suffolk County Happy Landing Fund, Inc.
c/o Peter Opromolla
Box 383
St. James, NY 11780
(516) 366-4843

Decription: Financial assistance to police officers and their families in Suffolk County, New York. Grants or loans given only to police officers in extreme financial difficulties
Restrictions: Limited to police officers in Suffolk County, New York
$ Given: In FY90, three grants of $1,000 each were awarded to individuals.
Application Information: Initial approach must be made by a superior officer. Formal application required; interviews required. Write or call for informational brochure.
Deadline: None
Contact: N/A

Otto Sussman Trust
P.O. Box 1374
Trainsmeadow Station
Flushing, NY 11370-9998
phone: N/A

Description: Financial assistance for medical bills and caregiving expenses to individuals with serious or terminal illnesses
Restrictions: Limited to residents of New York, New Jersey, Oklahoma, and Pennsylvania
$ Given: Grants range from $329 - $4,000.
Application Information: Write letter requesting application form and guidelines; explain circumstances of need; formal application required
Deadline: None
Contact: Edward S. Miller, Trustee

• • • • • • • • • • • • • • • • • • •

VonderLinden Charitable Trust
c/o Leonard Rachmilowitz
26 Mill Street
Rhinebeck, NY 12572
(914) 876-3021

Description: Grants for financially distressed residents of upstate New York. Funds may be used to meet a variety of needs, including medical bills.
Restrictions: Limited to residents of upstate New York
$ Given: In FY89, 101 grants totaling $23,262 were awarded to individuals; range, $4 - $538.
Application Information: Write or call for guidelines
Deadline: None
Contact: Leonard Rachmilowitz

OHIO

Christian BusinessCares Foundation
P.O. Box 360691
Cleveland, OH 44136
(216) 621-0096

Description: One-time grants for life-threatening medical emergencies
Restrictions: Limited to residents of northeast Ohio. Awards determined on basis of the effect of grant on applicant's overall condition.
$ Given: Grants range from $8 - $10,000; average, $270.
Application Information: Write for guidelines, brochure and newsletter; formal application required; interviews required
Deadline: None
Contact: N/A

Columbus Female Benevolent Society
228 South Drexel Avenue
Columbus, OH 43209
phone: N/A

Description: Direct aid to pensioned widows
Restrictions: Limited to widows who are residents of Franklin County, Ohio.
$ Given: In 1989, an unspecified number of grants totaling $32,800 were awarded to individuals.
Application Information: No direct applications; recipients are referred by people in the community who are familiar with their circumstances
Deadline: N/A
Contact: N/A

**The Ford (S.N. Ford &
Ada) Fund**
c/o Society Bank & Trust
P.O. Box 849
Mansfield, OH 44901
(419) 525-7676

Description: Grants for hospitalization and care of the aged and incurably ill
Restrictions: Limited to residents of Richland County, Ohio
$ Given: Grants range from $23 - $11,472.
Application Information: Write for guidelines and annual report
Deadline: N/A
Contact: Nick Gesouras, Regional Trust Officer

**Meshech Frost
Testamentary Trust**
109 South Washington
Street, Tiffin, OH 44883
phone: N/A

Description: Grants to Tiffin, Ohio residents who are in financial need
Restrictions: Limited to residents of Tiffin, Ohio
$ Given: Grants range from $169 - $690.
Application Information: Submit letter stating reasons for request
Deadline: None
Contact: Kenneth H. Myers, Secretary-Treasurer

**Virginia Wright Mothers
Guild, Inc.**
426 Clinton Street
Columbus, OH 43202-2741
phone: N/A

Description: Grants to aged women in financial need
Restrictions: Strictly limited to female residents of Columbus, Ohio
$ Given: Grants totaling $9,924 are awarded to individuals.
Application Information: Write for guidelines
Deadline: N/A
Contact: M. Courtwright

PRIVATE FOUNDATION FUNDING

• • • • • • • • • • • • • • • • • • • •

OKLAHOMA

Otto Sussman Trust
P.O. Box 1374
Trainsmeadow Station
Flushing, NY 11370-9998
phone: N/A

Description: Financial assistance for medical bills and caregiving expenses to individuals with serious or terminal illnesses
Restrictions: Limited to residents of New York, New Jersey, Oklahoma, and Pennsylvania
$ Given: Grants range from $329 - $4,000.
Application Information: Write letter requesting application form and guidelines; explain circumstances of need; formal application required
Deadline: None
Contact: Edward S. Miller, Trustee

OREGON

The Elizabeth Church Clarke Testamentary Trust/Fund Foundation
U.S. National Bank of Oregon
P.O. Box 3168
Portland, OR 97208
(503) 228-9405
APPLICATION ADDRESS:
Scottish Rite Temple, 709 S.W. 15th Avenue, Portland, OR 97205

Description: Grants for medical assistance. Payments may be made directly to the individuals or to the physicians and hospitals providing services.
Restrictions: Limited to residents of Oregon
$ Given: In 1989, total giving was $32,770.
Application Information: Initial approach by letter, detailing needs and costs
Deadline: None
Contact: G.L. Selmyhr, Executive Secretary

Clarke (Louis G. & Elizabeth L.) Endowment Fund
U.S. National Bank of Oregon
P.O. Box 3168
Portland, OR 97208
(503) 228-9405
APPLICATION ADDRESS:
Scottish Rite Temple, 709 S.W. 15th Avenue, Portland, OR 97205

Description: Grants to needy Masons or their immediate family who require hospitalization in the Portland, Oregon metropolitan area (Multnomah, Clackamas and Washington counties)
Restrictions: Limited to Masons and their immediate families
$ Given: In FY89, an unspecified number of grants totaling $34,381 were awarded to individuals.
Application Information: Write for guidelines
Deadline: N/A
Contact: G.L. Selmyhr, Executive Secretary

Blanche Fischer Foundation
1001 South West Fifth Avenue
Suite 1550
Portland, OR 97204
(503) 323-9111

Description: Financial aid for physically handicapped persons in Oregon
Restrictions: Limited to Oregon residents who have demonstrated financial need and who are disabled or physically handicapped
$ Given: In 1989, 148 grants totaling $70,187 were awarded to individuals; range, $25 - $1,500; general range, $100 - $1,000; average, $410.
Application Information: Write for application guidelines; formal application required
Deadline: None
Contact: William K. Shepherd, President

Sophia Byers McComas Foundation
c/o U.S. National Bank of Oregon
P.O. Box 3168
Portland, OR 97208
(503) 275-6564

Description: Grants to elderly and indigent residents of Oregon who are not receiving welfare assistance
Restrictions: Limited to residents of Oregon
$ Given: In FY89, an unspecified number of grants totaling $72,222 were awarded to individuals.
Application Information: Individuals may not apply directly; applicants are recommended to the trustees by various church groups, service agencies, etc.
Deadline: N/A
Contact: U.S. National Bank of Oregon, Trustee

Scottish Rite Oregon Consistory Almoner Fund, Inc.
Scottish Rite Temple
709 S.W. 15th Avenue
Portland, OR 97205
(503) 228-9405

Description: Assistance to financially distressed Masons and their families to help meet medical expenses
Restrictions: Limited to Masons, and their wives, widows and children who are residents of the state of Oregon
$ Given: In FY89, an unspecified number of grants totaling $19,437 were awarded to individuals.
Application Information: Write for guidelines
Deadline: None
Contact: Walter Peters

PRIVATE FOUNDATION FUNDING

• • • • • • • • • • • • • • • • • • •

PENNSYLVANIA

Margaret Baker Memorial Fund Trust
Mellon Bank (East) N.A.
P.O. Box 7236
Philadelphia, PA 19101-7236
phone: N/A
APPLICATION ADDRESS:
P.O. Box 663, Phoenixville,
PA 19460

Description: Financial aid to widows and single women over age 30 and handicapped children under age 14.
Restrictions: Limited to residents of the Phoenixville, Pennsylvania, area
$ Given: Grants range from $108 - $750.
Application Information: Send a letter including the applicant's age, income, infirmity (if any), and other supportive material, plus the name of a person who can verify the request.
Deadline: Applications accepted throughout the year; awards are usually made in July and November.
Contact: L. Darlington Lessig, Treasurer

Addison H. Gibson Foundation
Six PPG Place
Suite 860
Pittsburgh, PA 15222
(412) 261-1611

Description: Funds to cover hospital and medical costs for individuals with, "correctible physical difficulties"
Restrictions: Limited to residents of western Pennsylvania, with emphasis on Allegheny County
$ Given: Grants range from $60 - $12,000.
Application Information: Applicants must be referred by a medical professional. Formal application required. Medical professional must provide name, age, sex, and address of person for whom funding is sought, describe the nature of recommended medical assistance and provide the name of the patient's primary physician. Grants are made directly to the medical professionals/institution providing services. Write for further information; formal application required; interviews required.
Deadline: None
Contact: Charlotte G. Kisseleff, Secretary

• •

Edward W. Helfrick
Senior Citizens Trust
400 Market Street
Sunbury, PA 17801
phone: N/A

Description: Grants to senior citizens of the 107th Legislative District in Pennsylvania who are in need as a result of fire or illness
Restrictions: See above
$ Given: Four grants of $500 each are awarded to individuals.
Application Information: Write for guidelines
Deadline: None
Contact: N/A

William B. Lake
Foundation
Fidelity Bank, N.A.
Broad & Walnut Streets
3 MBO
Philadelphia, PA 19109
(215) 985-7320

Description: Aid to individuals suffering from respiratory diseases
Restrictions: Limited to residents of the Philadelphia, Pennsylvania, area
$ Given: In FY90, an unspecified number of grants totaling $30,000 were awarded to individuals.
Application Information: Initial approach by letter; please include details of physical condition and supporting documents
Deadlines: May 1 and November 1
Contact: Maureen B. Evans, Secretary-Treasurer

Otto Sussman Trust
P.O. Box 1374
Trainsmeadow Station
Flushing, NY 11370-9998
phone: N/A

Description: Financial assistance for medical bills and caregiving expenses to individuals with serious or terminal illnesses
Restrictions: Limited to residents of New York, New Jersey, Oklahoma, and Pennsylvania
$ Given: Grants range from $329 - $4,000.
Application Information: Write letter requesting application form and guidelines; explain circumstances of need; formal application required
Deadline: None
Contact: Edward S. Miller, Trustee

PRIVATE FOUNDATION FUNDING

. . . .

RHODE ISLAND

Bristol Home for Aged Women
c/o Rhode Island
Hospital Trust Bank
One Hospital Trust Plaza
Providence, RI 02903
(401) 278-8752

Description: Financial aid for elderly, needy women.
Restrictions: Limited to residents of Bristol, Rhode Island
$ Given: In FY89, eight grants totaling $9,310 were awarded to individuals; range, $100 - $4,900.
Application Information: Initial approach by letter interview; letter should include costs and description of service needed.
Deadline: June 1
Contact: Mr. Shawn P. Buckless, Assistant Vice President

Robert B. Cranston/ Theophilus T. Pitman Fund
18 Market Square
Newport, RI 02840
(401) 847-4260

Description: Grants to the aged, temporarily indigent and indigent people of Newport County, Rhode Island. Funds for medical assistance, food, utilities, clothing and housing
Restrictions: Limited to residents of Newport County, Rhode Island
$ Given: In FY89, an unspecified number of grants totaling $6,850 were awarded to individuals.
Application Information: Interview or reference from a local welfare agency required
Deadline: None
Contact: The Reverend D.C. Hambly, Jr., Administrator

Inez Sprague Trust
c/o Rhode Island
Hospital Trust Bank
One Hospital Trust Plaza
Providence, RI 02903
(401) 278-8700

Description: Financial assistance and medical expenses for needy individuals.
Restrictions: Limited to residents of Rhode Island
$ Given: In FY89, 23 grants totaling $6,000 were awarded to individuals; range, $79 - $1,500
Application Information: Initial approach by letter
Deadline: None
Contact: Trustee

• • • • • • • • • • • • • • • • • • • •

SOUTH CAROLINA

Graham Memorial Fund
308 West Main Street,
Bennettsville, SC 29512
803) 479-6804

Description: Grants for medical assistance and general welfare
Restrictions: Limited to residents of Bennettsville, South Carolina
$ Given: In FY89, 37 grants totaling $11,200 were awarded to individuals; range, $200 - $500.
Application Information: Formal application required
Deadline: June 1
Contact: Chairman

TENNESSEE

State Industries Foundation
P.O. Box 307
Old Ferry Road
Ashland City, TN 37015
(615) 244-7040

Description: Financial assistance to needy individuals in Tennessee, including State Industries employees
Restrictions: Limited to residents of Tennessee
$ Given: Grants range from $1 - $400; average, $150.
Application Information: Write or call for guidelines
Deadline: None
Contact: Joseph P. Lanier, Manager

TEXAS

Dallas Cotton Exchange Trust
Dallas Cotton Exchange,
c/o Mr. Joe Ferguson,
Dixon Trust Company,
3141 Hood Street, Suite 600, Dallas, TX 75219
phone: N/A

Description: Financial aid to persons engaged or formerly engaged in the cotton merchandising business in Dallas, Texas, their employees and former employees, and the immediate families of the above — when they are unable to work or, if able to work, unable to earn a sufficient amount to meet their needs
Restrictions: See above
$ Given: Grants range from $1,750 - $3,300.
Application Information: Formal application required
Deadline: None
Contact: Joe Ferguson

PRIVATE FOUNDATION FUNDING

• • • • • • • • • • • • • • • • • • •

H.C. Davis Fund
P.O. Box 2239
San Antonio, TX 78298
phone: N/A

Description: Grants to assist sick Masons living in the 39th Masonic District of Texas
Restrictions: (see above)
$ Given: Grants range from $200 - $3,075.
Application Information: Write for guidelines
Deadline: None
Contact: N/A

The Kings Foundation
P.O. Box 27333
Austin, TX 78755
phone: N/A

Description: Grants to individuals in financial need
Restrictions: Intended primarily for residents of Texas
$ Given: Grants range from $50 - $250.
Application Information: Initial approach by letter
Deadline: N/A
Contact: N/A

VIRGINIA

A.C. Needles Trust Fund Hospital Care
c/o Dominion Trust Company
P.O. Box 13327
Roanoke, VA 24040
phone: N/A

Description: Grants for hospital care to financially distressed individuals
Restrictions: Limited to individuals in the Roanoke, Virginia area
$ Given: Grants range from $710 - $9,450.
Application Information: Write for guidelines
Deadline: N/A
Contact: N/A

• • • • • • • • • • • • • • • • •

WASHINGTON

G.M.L. Foundation, Inc.
P.O. Box 848
Port Angeles, WA 98362
phone: N/A

Description: Grants for individuals who need medical help
Restrictions: Limited to residents of Clallam County, Washington
$ Given: rants totaling $12,275 are awarded to individuals.
Application Information: Write for guidelines
Deadline: N/A
Contact: Graham Ralston, Secretary

George T. Welch Testamentary Trust
c/o Baker-Boyer National Bank
P.O. Box 1796
Walla Walla, WA 99362
(509) 525-2000

Description: Medical assistance for financially distressed individuals
Restrictions: Limited to residents of Walla Walla County, Washington
$ Given: In FY89, 29 welfare assistance grants totaling $21,984 were awarded to individuals; range, $53 - $1,500.
Application Information: Formal application required
Deadlines: February 20, May 20, August 20, November 20
Contact: Bettie Loiacono, Trust Officer

WEST VIRGINIA

Good Shepherd Foundation, Inc.
Route 4
Box 349
Kinston, NC 28501-9317
(919) 569-3241

Description: Financial assistance for medical expenses
Restrictions: Limited to residents of Trent Township, West Virginia
$ Given: Grants range from $1,130 - $2,500.
Application Information: Initial approach by letter; formal application required
Deadline: None
Contact: Sue White, Secretary-Treasurer

PRIVATE FOUNDATION FUNDING

· · · · · · · · · · · · · · · · · · ·

**Jamey Harless
Foundation, Inc.**
Drawer D
Gilbert, WV 25621
(304) 664-3227

Description: Loans and grants to financially distressed families
Restrictions: Limited to residents of the Gilbert, West Virginia, area
$ Given: Distress grants totaling $4,720 are awarded to individuals; distress loans totaling $5,600 are made to individuals.
Application Information: Initial approach by letter; formal application required
Deadline: None
Contact: Sharon Murphy, Secretary

WISCONSIN

Edward Rutledge Charity
P.O. Box 758
Chippewa Falls, WI 54729
(715) 723-6618

Description: Grants and loans to needy residents of Chippewa County, Wisconsin
Restrictions: (see above)
$ Given: In FY90, 235 relief assistance grants totaling $16,284 were awarded to individuals; range, $5-$600.
Application Information: Formal application required; interviews required
Deadline: July 1
Contact: John Frampton, President

PRIVATE FOUNDATION FUNDING , NO GEOGRAPHICAL RESTRICTIONS

Bendheim (Charles and Els) Foundation
One Parker Plaza
Fort Lee, NJ 07024
phone: N/A

Description: Grants to individuals for charitable purposes, including aid to the sick and destitute
Restrictions: Applicants must be Jewish and in need of financial assistance
$ Given: In 1989, total giving was $171,884.
Application Information: Write for guidelines
Deadline: N/A
Contact: N/A

• •

Broadcasters Foundation, Inc.
320 West 57th Street
New York, NY 10019
(212) 586-2000

Description: Grants to needy members of the broadcast industry and their families
Restrictions: Open only to members of the broadcast industry and their families
$ Given: Grants range from $1,800 - $2,400.
Application Information: Formal application required
Deadline: None
Contact: N/A

Island Memorial Medical Fund, Inc.
c/o Richard Purinon
Main Road
Washington Island, WI 54246
phone: N/A

Description: Financial assistance to help cover medical expenses for needy individuals. Funds paid directly to physicians or treatment facilities
$ Given: Grants range from $630 - $8,759.
Application Information: Write foundation for application guidelines and current deadline information
Deadline: Varies
Contact: N/A

Jockey Club Foundation
40 East 52nd Street
New York, NY 10022
(212) 371-5970

Description: Grants to financially distressed individuals who are legitimately connected with thoroughbred breeding and racing
Restrictions: See above
$ Given: In 1989, a total of $394,278 was awarded in grants to individuals.
Application Information: Write for program information and application guidelines.
Deadline: None
Contact: Nancy Colletti, Secretary to the Trustees

PRIVATE FOUNDATION FUNDING

. . . .

**Max Mainzer Memorial
Foundation, Inc.**
570 Seventh Avenue
Third Floor
New York, NY 10018
(212) 921-3865

Description: Grants to financially distressed members of
the American Jewish KC Fraternity or their widows
Restrictions: (see above)
$ Given: In FY89, 15 grants totaling $34,440 were
awarded to individuals; range, $250 - $4,200.
Application Information: Contact foundation for guidelines
Deadline: None
Contact: N/A

**NFL Alumni Foundation
Fund**
c/o Sigmund M. Hyman
P.O. Box 248
Stevenson, MD 21153-0248
(301) 486-5454

Description: Financial assistance to disabled former
National Football League alumni (prior to 1959),
including grants for death benefits and medical expenses
Restrictions: (see above)
$ Given: 24 grants totaling $144,420 are awarded to
individuals; eligible persons may receive grants that will
supplement their total annual income by up to $12,000,
with a $250/month minimum.
Application Information: Initial approach by letter
Deadline: None
Contact: N/A

Katharine C. Pierce Trust
c/o State Street Bank &
Trust Company
P.O. Box 351
Boston, MA 02101
(617) 654-3357

Description: Financial assistance for needy women.
Restrictions: (see above)
$ Given: In 1989, an unspecified number of grants
totaling $33,500 were awarded to individuals; range, $250
- $5,000; general range, $1,000 - $5,000.
Application Information: Initial approach by letter;
include personal history, needs and financial condition
Deadline: None
Contact: Robert W. Seymour, Trust Officer

Corporate/ Employee Grants

. . . .

This chapter contains information about companies and corporations that provide grants or loans for their employees or former employees.

As in the chapter on Private Foundation Funding, the material is organized by state. In some cases, where a corporation has offices in several states, the corporation is listed only under the state in which its headquarters are located. Unless specificied in the restrictions, this does *not* mean that monies are available only to employees within that state. Wherever possible, each listing includes a description of what the foundation funds, any restrictions, the total amount of money awarded annually, the number of grants or loans made annually, the range of monies given, the average size of an award, information on how to apply, deadline date(s), and name(s) of contact person(s).

If your company/corporation is not included in this chapter, check with an employee benefits representative or your personnel director to see if your company offers assistance in paying medical expenses.

CORPORATE/EMPLOYEE GRANTS

. . . .

ARRANGED BY STATE, ACCORDING TO CORPORATE LOCATION

ALABAMA

The Stockham (William H. & Kate F.) Foundation, Inc.
c/o Stockham Valves & Fittings, Inc.
4000 North Tenth Ave.
P.O. Box 10326
Birmingham, AL 35202
phone: N/A

Description: Need-based grants
Restrictions: Strictly limited to **Stockham Valves & Fittings, Inc.** employees, former employees, and their dependents
$ Given: Grants range from $150 - $9,555.
Application Information: Initial contact by letter
Deadline: None
Contact: Herbert Stockham, Chairman

CALIFORNIA

A.P. Giannini Foundation for Employees
c/o Bank of America
Personnel Relations
Department No. 3650
P.O. Box 37000
San Francisco, CA 94137
(415) 622-3706

Description: Relief grants to help cover medical bills and other emergency expenses.
Restrictions: Limited to **Bank of America** employees and their families, and to employees of Bank of America subsidiaries
$ Given: Grants range from $787 - $2,640.
Application Information: Submit letter of application, including reason for grant request, amount requested, and assessment of applicant's financial status
Deadline: None
Contact: N/A

Clorinda Giannini Memorial Benefit Fund
c/o Bank of America
Trust Department
P.O. Box 37121
San Francisco, CA 94137
(415) 622-3650

Description: Emergency assistance grants for illness, accident disability, surgery, medical and nursing care, hospitalization, financial difficulties, and loss of income.
Restrictions: Limited to **Bank of America** employees
$ Given: Grants range from $35 - $6,226; general range, $800 - $2,000.
Application Information: Initial contact by letter
Deadline: None
Contact: Susan Morales

. . . .

George S. Ladd Memorial Fund
c/o V.M. Edwards
633 Folsom Street
Room 420
San Francisco, CA 94107
phone: N/A

Description: Financial assistance grants, including funding for medical treatment.
Restrictions: Limited to elderly and retired employees of **Pacific Bell, Nevada Bell** and **Pacific Northwest Bell**
$ Given: Grants range from $1,271 - $4,450.
Application Information: Write for guidelines
Deadline: N/A
Contact: N/A

Pfaffinger Foundation
Times Mirror Square
Los Angeles, CA 90053
(213) 237-5743

Description: Need-based grants
Restrictions: Limited to employees and former employees of **The Times Mirror Company**
$ Given: Grants range from $13 - $40,553.
Application Information: Initial contact by letter; formal application required; final notification usually in one week after application is received
Deadline: None
Contact: James C. Kelly, President

Plitt Southern Theatres, Inc. Employees Fund
1801 Century Park East
Suite 1225
Los Angeles, CA 90067
phone: N/A

Description: Welfare assistance grants
Restrictions: Limited to employees of **Plitt Southern Theatres**
$ Given: Grants range from range, $199 - $10,068.
Application Information: Write for guidelines
Deadline: N/A
Contact: Joe S. Jackson, President

CONNECTICUT

AMAX Aid Fund, Inc.
AMAX Center
Greenwich, CT 06836
phone: N/A

Description: Financial assistance to needy employees, former employees, and families of deceased employees of **AMAX, Inc.** and its subsidiaries.
Restrictions: Individuals earning an annual salary from AMAX or receiving an AMAX pension are not eligible
$ Given: Four grants totaling $7,150 are awarded to individuals; no grants were awarded in 1988.
Application Information: Write for guidelines
Deadline: N/A
Contact: David George Ball, Senior Vice President

CORPORATE/EMPLOYEE GRANTS

· · · · · · · · · · · · · · · · · · ·

IDAHO

Morrison-Knudsen Employees Foundation, Inc.
One Morrison-Knudsen Plaza
Boise, ID 83729
(208) 386-5000

Description: Need-based assistance
Restrictions: Limited to employees of **Morrison-Knudsen**
$ Given: Grants range from $700 - $8,900.
Application Information: Write or call for guidelines
Deadline: None
Contact: M.M. Puckett, Foundation Manager

ILLINOIS

The Clara Abbott Foundation
One Abbott Park Road
Abbott Park, IL 60064-3500
(312) 937-1091

Description: Relief grants and loans to employees and retired employees of Abbott Laboratories, as well as to members of their families. Aid to aged and indigent individuals.
Restrictions: Limited to employees, retirees and families of employees of **Abbott Laboratories**
$ Given: 516 relief grants totaling $867,973 are awarded to individuals; 68 grants totaling $145,398 are awarded to the elderly; range, $60 - $10,800.
Application Information: Write or call for guidelines
Deadline: None
Contact: David C. Jefferies, Executive Director

Walgreen Benefit Fund
200 Wilmot Road
Deerfield, IL 60015
(708) 940-2931

Description: Welfare assistance grants
Restrictions: Limited to **Walgreen** employees and their families
$ Given: In FY90, an unspecified number of grants totaling $305,000 were awarded to individuals.
Application Information: Initial contact by letter
Deadline: None
Contact: Edward H. King, Vice President

• • • • • • • • • • • • • • • • • • •

MASSACHUSETTS

Charles F. Bacon Trust
c/o Bank of New England, N.A.
28 State Street
Boston, MA 02107
(617) 573-6416

Description: Assistance grants
Restrictions: Limited to former employees of **Conrad and Chandler Company** who have retired or resigned due to illness
$ Given: Grants range from $2,000 - $7,000.
Application Information: Initial contact by letter
Deadline: December 31
Contact: Kerry Herlilhy, Senior Vice President, Bank of New England

Henry Hornblower Fund, Inc.
Box 2365
Boston, MA 02169
(617) 589-3286

Description: Need-based grants
Restrictions: Limited to current and former employees of **Hornblower & Weeks**
$ Given: Grants range from $1,000 - $5,000.
Application Information: Initial contact by letter
Deadline: None
Contact: Nathan N. Withington, President

MICHIGAN

Hudson-Webber Foundation
333 West Fort Street
Suite 1310
Detroit, MI 48226
(313) 963-7777

Description: Counseling services and last-resort financial assistance. Grants provided primarily in cases involving problems with physical or emotional health, and in financial emergencies.
Restrictions: Limited to employees and qualified retired employees of the **J.L. Hudson Company**
$ Given: Grants range from $500 - $1,000.
Application Information: Formal application required for review by the foundation's trustees; interviews required
Deadline: None
Contact: Gilbert Hudson, President

CORPORATE/EMPLOYEE GRANTS

• • • • • • • • • • • • • • • • • •

MINNESOTA

CENEX Foundation
5500 Cenex Drive
Inver Grove Heights, MN
55075
(612) 451-5105

Description: Financial assistance grants
Restrictions: Limited to former employees of **CENEX** and its affiliates
$ Given: 33 welfare grants totaling $113,152 are awarded to individuals; range, $1,500 - $7,512.
Application Information: Initial contact by letter; formal application required
Deadline: None
Contact: N/A

MISSOURI

Butler Manufacturing Company Foundation
Penn Valley Park
P.O. Box 419917
BMA Tower
Kansas City, MO 64141-0197
(816) 968-3208

Description: Hardship grants to aid individuals in emergency financial distress due to serious illness, fire, or natural disaster.
Restrictions: Limited to **Butler Manufacturing Company** employees, retirees and their dependents
$ Given: Three hardship grants totaling $10,650 Grants range from awarded; range, $650 - $8,000; general range, $500 - $2,000
Application Information: Write for application guidelines and program information; interviews required
Deadline: None
Contact: Barbara Lee Fay, Foundation Administrator

Hall Family Foundations
c/o Charitable and Crown
Investment
Department 323
P.O. Box 419580
Kansas City, MO 64141-6580
(816) 274-8516

Description: Grants for emergency relief assistance
Restrictions: Strictly limited to employees of **Hallmark**
$ Given: Total giving is $1,716,987; relief assistance subtotal unspecified
Application Information: Write or call for guidelines
Deadline: N/A
Contact: Margaret H. Pence, Director/Program Officer

Kansas City Life Employees Welfare Fund
3520 Broadway
Kansas City, MO 64111-2565
(816) 753-7000

Description: Medical assistance grants
Restrictions: Limited to **Kansas City Life** employees and their spouses and/or dependents
$ Given: Two grants totaling $4,263 are awarded to individuals; range, $950 - $3,313
Application Information: Initial contact by letter
Deadline: None
Contact: Dennis M. Gaffney

David May Employees Trust Fund
Sixth and Olive Streets
St. Louis, MO 63101
phone: N/A

Description: Need-based grants
Restrictions: Limited to employees and former employees of the **May Department Stores Company**
$ Given: An unspecified number of grants totaling $11,500 are awarded to individuals
Application Information: Write for guidelines
Deadline: N/A
Contact: N/A

Edward F. Swinney Foundation
c/o Boatmen's First National Bank of Kansas City
P.O. Box 419038
Kansas City, MO 64183
(816) 234-7481

Description: Need-based grants
Restrictions: Limited to employees of **Boatmen's First National Bank of Kansas City**
$ Given: 138 grants totaling $52,826 are awarded to individuals; range, $9 - $5,621
Application Information: Formal application required
Deadline: None
Contact: David P. Ross, Trust Officer

NEVADA

George S. Ladd Memorial Fund
c/o V.M. Edwards
633 Folsom Street
Room 420
San Francisco, CA 94107
phone: N/A

Description: Financial assistance grants, including funding for medical treatment.
Restrictions: Limited to elderly and retired employees of **Pacific Bell, Nevada Bell** and **Pacific Northwest Bell**
$ Given: Five grants totaling $13,341 are awarded to individuals; range, $1,271 - $4,450
Application Information: Write for guidelines
Deadline: N/A
Contact: N/A

CORPORATE/EMPLOYEE GRANTS

. . . .

NEW JERSEY

Ittleson-Beaumont Fund
(*formerly Ittleson Beneficial Fund*)
c/o The C.I.T. Group
Holdings, Inc.
135 West 50th Street
New York, NY 10020
(212) 408-6000
APPLICATION ADDRESS:
650 CIT Drive, Livingston,
NJ 07039

Description: Need-based grants to provide supplemental income to individuals demonstrating continuing financial hardship.
Restrictions: Intended primarily, but not exclusively, for current and former employees of **C.I.T. Financial Corporation** and its affiliates, as well as for the families of employees
$ Given: Grants range from $285 - $18,000
Application Information: Submit application letter stating reason for request and providing details of applicant's financial status
Deadline: None
Contact: Clare Carmichael

NEW YORK

Cesare Barbieri Dixie Cup Employees Foundation Trust
c/o Bankers Trust Company
P.O. Box 829
Church Street Station
New York, NY 10008
APPLICATION ADDRESS:
280 Park Avenue, New York, NY 10017
(212) 850-2291

Description: Grants to Dixie Cup Company employees and their beneficiaries, to provide tax-exempt benefits.
Restrictions: Limited to employees of **Dixie Cup Company** and their beneficiaries
$ Given: Grants range from $14 - $585
Application Information: Write or call for guidelines
Deadline: N/A
Contact: Margery Finnin, Trust Officer

Richard D. Brown Trust B
c/o Chemical Bank
Administrative Services
Department
30 Rockefeller Plaza
New York, NY 10112
(212) 621-2143

Description: Need-based loans
Restrictions: Limited to employees of **Chemical Bank**
$ Given: An unspecified number of loans to individuals totaling $10,722 are made
Application Information: Recipients chosen by staff benefits committee
Deadline: None
Contact: Mrs. B. Strohmeier

The Ernst & Young Foundation
(formerly The Ernst & Whinney Foundation)
277 Park Avenue
New York, NY 10172
phone: N/A

Description: Financial assistance grants to employees and their families.
Restrictions: Limited to **Ernst & Young** employees and their families
$ Given: One relief grant for $2,400 is awarded
Application Information: Write for guidelines
Deadline: N/A
Contact: Bruce J. Mantia, Administrator

Ittleson-Beaumont Fund
(*formerly Ittleson Beneficial Fund*)
c/o The C.I.T. Group Holdings, Inc.
135 West 50th Street
New York, NY 10020
(212) 408-6000
APPLICATION ADDRESS:
650 CIT Drive, Livingston, NJ 07039

Description: Need-based grants to provide supplemental income to individuals demonstrating continuing financial hardship.
Restrictions: Intended primarily, but not exclusively, for current and former employees of **C.I.T. Financial Corporation** and its affiliates, as well as for the families of employees
$ Given: Grants range from $285 - $18,000
Application Information: Submit application letter stating reason for request and providing details of applicant's financial status
Deadline: None
Contact: Clare Carmichael

Glenn L. Martin Foundation
c/o Fiduciary Trust Company of New York
Two World Trade Center
New York, NY 10048
(212) 466-4100

Description: Welfare assistance grants
Restrictions: Limited to retired employees of the **Martin Marietta Corporation**
$ Given: Grants range from $100 - $2,500
Application Information: Write or call for guidelines
Deadline: N/A
Contact: N/A

CORPORATE/EMPLOYEE GRANTS

• • • • • • • • • • • • • • • • • • • •

McCrory Corporation Needy & Worthy Employees Trust
c/o Chase Manhattan Bank
Tax Services Division
1211 Avenue of the Americas
36th Floor
New York, NY 10036
phone: N/A

Description: Need-based grants
Restrictions: Limited to worthy employees of the **McCrory Corporation**
$ Given: Grants range from $5,000 - $7,444
Application Information: Write for guidelines
Deadline: N/A
Contact: Larry Tynan

United Merchants & Manufacturers Employees Welfare Foundation
1407 Broadway
6th Floor
New York, NY 10018-5103
phone: N/A

Description: Need-based grants
Restrictions: Limited to current and former employees of **United Merchants & Manufacturers, Inc.**, and to members of their families
$ Given: Grants range from $375 - $825
Application Information: Write for guidelines
Deadline: None
Contact: Lawrence Marx, Jr., Trustee

NORTH CAROLINA

Burlington Industries Foundation
P.O. Box 21207
3330 West Friendly Avenue
Greensboro, NC 27420
(919) 379-2515

Description: Emergency grants designed to aid individuals who have experienced severe loss from disaster.
Restrictions: Limited to **Burlington Industries** employees and their families; primary focus of giving in North Carolina, South Carolina and Virginia
$ Given: Grants range from $250 - $1,000
Application Information: Call or write for program information; interviews upon request
Deadline: None
Contact: Park R. Davidson, Executive Director

• • • • • • • • • • • • • • • • • •

OHIO

National Machinery Foundation, Inc.
Greenfield Street
P.O. Box 747
Tiffin, OH 44883
(419) 447-5211

Description: Need-based grants
Restrictions: Limited to former employees of **National Machinery** and to other financially distressed individuals in Seneca County, Ohio
$ Given: Grants range from $150 - $4,000
Application Information: Initial contact by letter
Deadline: N/A
Contact: D.B. Bero, Administrator

Richman Brothers Foundation
Box 657
Chagrin Falls, OH 44022
(216) 247-5426

Description: Relief assistance grants
Restrictions: Limited to employees, pensioners, widows, and children of employees of the **Richman Brothers Company**; preference to individuals in Cleveland, Ohio
$ Given: Grants range from $100 - $1,995
Application Information: Write for guidelines; formal application required
Deadline: November 15
Contact: Richard R. Moore, President

OREGON

Journal Publishing Company Employees Welfare Fund, Inc.
P.O. Box 3168
Portland, OR 97208
phone: N/A

Description: Welfare assistance grants
Restrictions: Limited to employees of **Journal Publishing Company**
$ Given: Grants range from $1,200 - $3,600
Application Information: Write for guidelines
Deadline: None
Contact: N/A

CORPORATE/EMPLOYEE GRANTS

• • • • • • • • • • • • • • • • • • •

George S. Ladd Memorial Fund
c/o V.M. Edwards
633 Folsom Street
Room 420
San Francisco, CA 94107
phone: N/A

Description: Financial assistance grants, including funding for medical treatment.
Restrictions: Limited to elderly and retired employees of **Pacific Bell, Nevada Bell** and **Pacific Northwest Bell**
$ Given: Grants range from $1,271 - $4,450
Application Information: Write for guidelines
Deadline: N/A
Contact: N/A

PENNSYLVANIA

Vang Memorial Foundation
P.O. Box 11727
Pittsburgh, PA 15228
(412) 563-0261

Description: Grants-in-aid
Restrictions: Limited to past, present and future employees of **George Vang, Inc.** and related companies, and their dependents
$ Given: 15 grants totaling $29,233 are awarded to individuals; range, $670 - $5,251; general range, $720 - $2,000
Application Information: Submit introductory letter, including name, address and telephone number of applicant and specifying type of grant requested and basis of need
Deadline: None
Contact: E.J. Hosko, Treasurer

SOUTH CAROLINA

Burlington Industries Foundation
P.O. Box 21207
3330 West Friendly Avenue
Greensboro, NC 27420
(919) 379-2515

Description: Emergency grants designed to aid individuals who have experienced severe loss from disaster.
Restrictions: Limited to **Burlington Industries** employees and their families; primary focus of giving in North Carolina, South Carolina and Virginia
$ Given: Grants range from $250 - $1,000
Application Information: Call or write for program information; interviews upon request
Deadline: None
Contact: Park R. Davidson, Executive Director

TEXAS

Amon G. Carter Star Telegram Employees Fund
P.O. Box 17480
Fort Worth, TX 76102
(817) 332-3535

Description: Medical/hardship assistance and pension supplements
Restrictions: Limited to employees of the **Fort Worth Star-Telegram**, **KXAS-TV**, and **WBAP-Radio**
$ Given: 28 welfare assistance grants totaling $233,017 are awarded; range, $844 - $7,964
Application Information: Initial contact by letter
Deadline: None
Contact: Nenetta Tatum, President

VIRGINIA

Burlington Industries Foundation
P.O. Box 21207
3330 West Friendly Avenue
Greensboro, NC 27420
(919) 379-2515

Description: Emergency grants designed to aid individuals who have experienced severe loss from disaster.
Restrictions: Limited to **Burlington Industries** employees and their families; primary focus of giving in North Carolina, South Carolina and Virginia
$ Given: Grants range from $250 - $1,000
Application Information: Call or write for program information; interviews upon request
Deadline: None
Contact: Park R. Davidson, Executive Director

WASHINGTON

George S. Ladd Memorial Fund
c/o V.M. Edwards
633 Folsom Street
Room 420
San Francisco, CA 94107
phone: N/A

Description: Financial assistance grants, including funding for medical treatment.
Restrictions: Limited to elderly and retired employees of **Pacific Bell, Nevada Bell** and **Pacific Northwest Bell**
$ Given: Grants range from $1,271 - $4,450
Application Information: Write for guidelines
Deadline: N/A
Contact: N/A

CORPORATE/EMPLOYEE GRANTS

• • • • • • • • • • • • • • • • • • • •

COMPANIES WITH EMPLOYEES NATIONWIDE AND ABROAD

The Correspondents Fund
c/o Rosenman & Cohen
575 Madison Avenue
New York, NY 10022-2511
phone: N/A
APPLICATION ADDRESS: c/
o The New York Times, 229
West 43rd Street, New
York, NY 10036

Description: Emergency grants
Restrictions: Limited to individuals who have worked in the U.S. press, television, radio, news, film, and other U.S. organizations within or outside the U.S., and to individuals who have worked in the foreign press or other foreign news organizations, and to their dependents
$ Given: Grants range from $2,500 - $3,000
Application Information: Submit an introductory letter, including details of the circumstances for which aid is requested
Deadline: None
Contact: James L. Greenfield, President

The Crane Fund
202 West Adams Street
Room 849
Chicago, IL 60606
phone: N/A

Description: Need-based grants
Restrictions: Open to former employees of **Crane Company** in the U.S. and Great Britain
$ Given: 1,366 grants totaling $1,646,392 are awarded to individuals
Application Information: Write for guidelines
Deadline: None
Contact: Fern N. Brodie, Senior Caseworker

Roger L. Von Amelunxen Foundation, Inc.
83-21 Edgerton Boulevard
Jamaica, NY 11432
(718) 641-4800

Description: Welfare assistance grants
Restrictions: Limited to financially distressed families of **U.S. Customs Service** employees
$ Given: In FY89, nine welfare assistance grants totaling $21,000 were awarded to individuals; range, $500 - $5,000
Application Information: Submit letter with proof of relationship to U.S. Customs Service employee
Deadline: August 1
Contact: Karen Donnelly, Vice President

Flow-through Funding

· ·

Many foundations will give monies to individuals indirectly; that is, individuals must apply under the auspices of nonprofit organizations. Grants are paid directly to medical institutions or organizations for the benefit of individuals in financial need. The nonprofit organization acts as the individual's sponsor or parent organization. The monies awarded are paid directly to the nonprofit organization, which passes them along to the individual. This is known as *flow-through* funding. Usually the nonprofit organization receives a fee of three to seven percent (3% - 7%) of monies raised. There is *no* up-front fee paid to the sponsor/parent organization. The three to seven percent fee is customary; it is not an obligation.

How do you go about finding a nonprofit conduit? Check any local directory of nonprofit organizations (your local library will usually have such directories in its collection, perhaps in a community services section). Contact local citywide consortium-styled associations operating in your area of interest, such as the United Way, health planning bodies, federations, and so on. Speak to their directors or public information officers and elicit their suggestions for possible sponsors. Also check national organizational reference books, such as the *Encyclopedia of Associations*, for other potential candidates.

FLOW-THROUGH FUNDING

. . . .

ALABAMA

The Greater Birmingham Foundation
P.O. Box 131027
Birmingham, AL 32513
(205) 933-0753

Description: Promotes the health, welfare, cultural, educational, and social needs of the Birmingham area
$ Given: $1,505,875 for grants
Application: Initial approach by letter
Deadline: None
Contact: Mrs. William McDonald, Jr., Executive Director

Hargis (Estes H. and Florence Parker) Charitable Foundation
317 20th Street North
P.O. Box 370404
Birmingham, AL 35237
(205) 251-2881

Description: Funding for health and youth services
$ Given: Seven grants totaling $395,374; range, $300-$376,075
Areas of Support: Alabama, Tennessee
Application: Initial approach by letter
Deadline: May 1
Contact: Gerald D. Colvin, Jr., Chair

D.W. McMillan Foundation
329 Belleville Avenue
P.O. Box 867
Brewton, AL 36427
(205) 867-4881

Description: Funds local health and welfare organizations (limited to programs giving direct aid)
$ Given: 21 grants totaling $392,000; range, $1,500-$60,000
Areas of Support: Escambia County, Alabama, and Escambia County, Florida
Application: Initial approach by letter
Deadline: December 1
Contact: James D. Nabors, Secretary-Treasurer

Monsanto Fund
800 North Lindbergh
Boulevard
St. Louis, MO 63167
(314) 694-4596

Description: Funding interests include health services, hospitals, social services, youth, education (science and mathematics), and community funds
$ Given: Grants totaling $8,285,748; range, $100-$1,112,000
Areas of Support: Alabama, California, Florida, Georgia, Idaho, Illinois, Massachusetts, Maine, Missouri, New Jersey, North Carolina, Ohio, South Carolina, Texas, and West Virginia
Application: Proposal
Deadline: None
Contact: John L. Mason, President

ALASKA

FHP Foundation
401 East Ocean Boulevard
Suite 206
Long Beach, CA 90802
(310) 590-8655

Description: Funds direct delivery of health care services, including education programs, programs for the elderly and chronically ill, and primary care projects in underserved areas.
$ Given: 17 grants totaling $773,064; range, $2,900-$89,000
Application: Initial approach by letter
Deadline: February 15, May 15, August 15, and November 15
Contact: Sandra Lund Gavin, Executive Director

Meyer Memorial Trust
1515 S.W. Fifth Avenue
Suite 500
Portland, OR 97201
(503) 228-5512

Description: General purpose grants in Oregon for education, health and social welfare, arts and humanities; special program grants for Aging and Independence and Support for Children at Risk in Oregon, Alaska, Idaho, Montana, and Washington; operates a Small Grants Program ($500-$8,000) for small projects in Oregon
$ Given: 209 grants totaling $11,953,746; range, $500-$2,000,000
Application: Application form required
Deadline: April 1, October 1 for Aging and Independence; July 15, October 15 for Small Grants Program; no deadline for general purpose grants
Contact: Charles S. Rooks, Executive Director

FLOW-THROUGH FUNDING

• • • • • • • • • • • • • • • • • • • •

ARIZONA

Arizona Community Foundation
4350 East Camelback Road
Suite 216 C
Phoenix, AZ 85018
(602) 952-9954

Description: Funds children's mental health, youth agencies, health agencies, organizations for the handicapped, and other human services programs
$ Given: 182 grants totaling $2,017,865; average range, $1,000-$10,000
Application: Initial approach by letter or telephone
Deadlines: February 1, June 1, October 1
Contact: Steven D. Mittenthal, President

FHP Foundation
401 East Ocean Boulevard
Suite 206
Long Beach, CA 90802
(310) 590-8655

Description: Funds direct delivery of health care services, including education programs, programs for the elderly and chronically ill, and primary care projects in underserved areas
$ Given: 17 grants totaling $773,064; range, $2,900-$89,000
Areas of Support: Giving in southern California, Utah, New Mexico, and Arizona
Application: Initial approach by letter
Deadline: February 15, May 15, August 15, and November 15
Contact: Sandra Lund Gavin, Executive Director

ARKANSAS

Arkansas Community Foundation, Inc.
604 East 6th Street
Little Rock, AR 72202
(501) 372-1116

Description: Areas of support include health, community development, social services, and education
$ Given: Grants totaling $958,642
Application: Initial approach by letter or telephone
Deadlines: January 1, April 1, September 1, and October 1
Contact: Martha Ann Jones, Executive Director

● ● ● ● ● ● ● ● ● ● ● ● ● ● ● ● ● ● ● ●

Arkla Corporate Giving Program
400 East Capitol Avenue
P.O. Box 751
Little Rock, AR 72203
(501) 377-4610

Description: Funds a wide variety of programs, including health services, mental health, AIDS, child welfare and drug abuse
$ Given: N/A
Limitations: Giving in major operating areas (Arkansas, California, Kansas, Texas, Oklahoma, and Mississippi)
Application: Initial approach by letter
Deadline: None
Contact: James L. Rutherford III, Senior Vice President (Little Rock, Arkansas area) or Hugh H. McCastlain (Shreveport, Louisiana area)

The Walton (Sam M. and Helen R.) Foundation
125 West Central
No. 210
Bentonville, Arkansas 72712
(501) 273-5743

Description: Funds health services, education, youth programs, social services, and religious support
$ Given: Grants totaling $440,633; high, $100,000
Application: Initial approach by letter or telephone
Deadline: None
Contact: Jan Ney

CALIFORNIA

The Annenberg Fund, Inc.
St. Davids Center
150 Radnor Chester Road
Suite A 200
St. Davids, PA 19087
(215) 341-9270

Description: Funding interests include education, health and medical research, community service, and cultural programs
$ Given: 150 grants totaling $6,020,616; range, $100-$1,666,667
Areas of Support: Pennsylvania, California, New York
Application: Applications not accepted; giving to pre-selected organizations
Deadline: N/A
Contact: Alice C. Cory, Secretary-Treasurer

FLOW-THROUGH FUNDING

. . . .

Argyros Foundation
950 South Coast Drive
Suite 200
Costa Mesa, CA 92626
(714) 241-5000

Description: Funds education, religious giving, social services, recreation, and health services
$ Given: 90 grants totaling $915,000; range, $50-$145,000
Application: Proposal
Deadline: June 1
Contact: Chuck Packard, Trustee

The Bialis Family Foundation
c/o Melveny and Meyers
1800 Century Park East
Suite 600
Los Angeles, CA 90067
(213) 553-6700

Description: Funds social services, education, health services, and Jewish organizations
$ Given: 38 grants totaling $204,373; range, $500-$15,000
Application: Applications not accepted; giving to pre-selected organizations
Deadline:N/A
Contact: N/A

Community Foundation of Santa Clara County
960 West Hedding
No. 220
San Jose, CA 95126
(408) 241-2666

Description: Funding includes health and social services
$ Given: 300 grants totaling $1,471,969; average range, $2,500-$15,000
Application: Initial approach by letter
Deadline: N/A
Contact: Peter Hero, Executive Director

The Mary A. Crocker Trust
233 Post Street
Second Floor
San Francisco, CA 94108
(415) 982-0139

Description: Funds child welfare, social services, women's projects, education, health services, and community development
$ Given: 48 grants totaling $490,080; range, $3,000-$50,000
Application: Initial approach by letter
Deadline: None
Contact: Barbaree Jernigan, Administrator

• • • • • • • • • • • • • • • • • •

Freeman E. Fairfield Foundation
3610 Long Beach Boulevard
P.O. Box 7798
Long Beach, CA 90807
(310) 427-7219

Description: Supports youth agencies, medical centers and clinics, handicapped and general social services, including the aged and child welfare and development
$ Given: 20 grants totaling $378,486; average range, $5,000-$20,000
Application: Initial approach by letter
Deadline: May 1
Contact: Edna E. Sellers, Trustee

Fannie Mae Foundation
3900 Wisconsin Avenue NW
Washington, DC 20016
(202) 752-6500

Description: Funding interests include housing and community development, and health and social concerns
$ Given: 300 grants totaling $1,151,567; range, $100-$50,000
Areas of Support: Washington, DC; Pasadena, California; Atlanta, Georgia; Chicago, Illinois; and Philadelphia, Pennsylvania
Application: Proposal
Deadline: None
Contact: Harriet M. Ivey, Executive Director

The Favrot Fund
909 Wirt Road
No. 101
Houston, TX 77024
(713) 956-4009

Description: Focus on community-based programs directed toward health, the needy, and the arts
$ Given: 24 grants totaling $310,000; range, $2,000-$25,000
Areas of Support: Texas, California, New York, and Washington, DC
Application: Initial approach by letter
Deadline: None
Contact: Mrs. Carol Parker

FHP Foundation
401 East Ocean Boulevard
Suite 206
Long Beach, CA 90802
(310) 590-8655

Description: Funds direct delivery of health care services, including education programs, programs for the elderly and chronically ill, and primary care projects in underserved areas
$ Given: 17 grants totaling $773,064; range, $2,900-$89,000
Areas of Support: Giving in southern California, Utah, New Mexico, and Arizona
Application: Initial approach by letter
Deadline: February 15, May 15, August 15, and November 15
Contact: Sandra Lund Gavin, Executive Director

59

FLOW-THROUGH FUNDING

. . . .

First Nationwide Bank Corporate Giving Program
700 Market Street
San Francisco, CA 94102
(415) 772-1575

Description: Funds community, social, and health services
$ Given: 220 grants totaling $305,000; range, $150-$20,000
Application: Application form not required; write for guidelines
Deadline: None
Contact: Stephen L. Johnson, Senior Vice President

The Garland (John Jewett and H. Chandler) Foundation
P.O. Box 550
Pasadena, CA 91102

Description: Funds social services for the elderly, youth agencies, hospitals and health services
$ Given: 50 grants totaling $1,261,500; average range, $5,000-$20,000
Application: Initial approach by letter
Deadline: None
Contact: N/A

The Fred Gellert Foundation
1655 Southgate Avenue
Suite 203
Daly City, CA 94015
(415) 991-1855

Description: Funds cultural programs, hospitals, health care programs, programs for the disabled, and social service agencies
$ Given: 95 grants totaling $649,733; range, $300-$100,000
Areas of Support: Giving in San Francisco and San Mateo counties, California
Application: Initial approach by letter
Deadline: None
Contact: Fred Gellert, Jr., Chairman

The William G. Gilmore Foundation
120 Montgomery Street
Suite 1880
San Francisco, CA 94104
(415) 546-1400

Description: Funds community-based organization, including family and social services, health services, and AIDS programs
$ Given: 132 grants totaling $766,345; range, $200-$50,000
Areas of Support: Giving in northern California, Oregon, and Washington
Application: Initial approach by letter
Deadlines: May 1, November 1
Contact: Faye Wilson, Secretary

• • • • • • • • • • • • • • • • • • • •

Great American Corporate Giving Program
600 B Street, Suite 800
San Diego, CA 92101
(619) 231-6242

Description: Funds community health care, education, and the arts
$ Given: N/A
Application: Initial approach by letter
Deadline: None
Contact: Karen Miller, Community Relations Officer

Hedco Foundation
c/o Fitzgerald, Abbott and Beardsley
1221 Broadway
21st Floor
Oakland, CA 94612

Description: Funds educational and health service institutions
$ Given: 23 grants totaling $1,019,454; range, $500-$469,160
Application: Proposal
Deadline: None
Contact: Mary A. Goriup, Foundation Manager

The James Irvine Foundation
One Market Plaza
Spear Tower, Suite 1715
San Francisco, CA 94105
(415) 644-1362

Description: Funds private higher education, health associations and services, including AIDS programs
$ Given: 273 grants totaling $20,487,000; average range, $25,000-$750,000
Application: Initial approach by letter
Deadline: None
Contact: Luz A. Vega, Director of Grants Program

Irvine Health Foundation
4199 Campus Drive
Suite 550
Irvine, CA 92715
(714) 854-6484

Description: Funds community health care; supports research on health care systems and programs, health programs and clinics (including a senior care center and drug abuse programs)
$ Given: 10 grants totaling $913,441; range, $2,500-$300,000
Areas of Support: Orange County, California
Application: Initial approach by letter
Deadline: None
Contact: Edward B. Kaie, Executive Director

FLOW-THROUGH FUNDING

• •

Jerome Foundation
2660 West Woodland Drive
Suite 160
Anaheim, CA 92801
(714) 995-1696

Description: Funds medical research, services for handicapped children and the blind, and hospitals and health services
$ Given: 17 grants totaling $147,383; range, $100-$124,534
Application: Form not required
Deadline: None
Contact: Pat Perry

George Frederick Jewett Foundation
One Maritime Plaza
Suite 990
San Francisco, CA 94111
(415) 421-1351

Description: Interests include health care and medical research and services
$ Given: 134 grants totaling $953,597; range, $500-$25,000
Areas of Support: San Francisco, California; eastern Washington; northern Idaho
Application: Initial approach by letter
Deadlines: February 15, May 15, August 15, and November 1
Contact: Theresa A. Mullen, Program Director

Livingston Memorial Foundation
625 North A Street
Oxnard, CA 93030
(805) 983-0561

Description: Funding support for health and health-related activites
$ Given: 27 grants totaling $313,750; range, $840-$165,000
Areas of Support: Ventura County, California
Application: Initial approach by letter
Deadline: February 1
Contact: Laura K. McAvoy

Bert William Martin Foundation
c/o The Northern Trust Company
50 South LaSalle Street
Chicago, Illinois 60675
(312) 630-6000

Description: Funds hospitals and health services
$ Given: 23 grants totaling $147,700; range, $300-$75,000
Areas of Support: California and Mount Vernon, Ohio
Application: Applications not accepted; giving to pre-selected organizations
Deadline: N/A
Contact: N/A

• • • • • • • • • • • • • • • • • • • •

**The Milken Family
Foundation**
c/o Foundations of the
Milken Families
15250 Ventura Boulevard
Second Floor
Sherman Oaks, CA 91403

Description: Interests include health care and medical research, and to make the benefits of both basic and highly advanced health care available to those who need them
$ Given: Grants totaling $4,015,074; range, $100-$500,000
Application: Applications not accepted; giving to pre-selected organizations
Deadline: N/A
Contact: Dr. Jules Lesner, Executive Director

**The Milken Family
Medical Foundation**
c/o Foundations of the
Milken Families
15250 Ventura Boulevard
Second Floor
Sherman Oaks, CA 91403

Description: Interests include health care and medical research, and to make the benefits of both basic and highly advanced health care available to those who need them
$ Given: 68 grants totaling $4,524,310; range, $180-$950,000
Application: Applications not accepted; giving to pre-selected organizations
Deadline: N/A
Contact: Lori Milken, President

Monsanto Fund
800 North Lindbergh
Boulevard
St. Louis, Missouri 63167
(314) 694-4596

Description: Funding interests include health services, hospitals, social services, youth, education (science and mathematics), and community funds
$ Given: Grants totaling $8,285,748; range, $100-$1,112,000
Areas of Support: Alabama, California, Florida, Georgia, Idaho, Illinois, Massachusetts, Maine, Missouri, New Jersey,
North Carolina, Ohio, South Carolina, Texas, and West Virginia
Application: Proposal
Deadline: None
Contact: John L. Mason, President

FLOW-THROUGH FUNDING

. . . .

The Norris (Kenneth T. and Eileen L.) Foundation
11 Golden Shore
Suite 440
Long Beach, CA 90802
(310) 435-8444

Description: Funds hospitals, health services, medical research, and social services
$ Given: 121 grants totaling $3,286,800; range, $1,000-$625,000
Application: Initial approach by letter
Deadline: None
Contact: Ronald R. Barnes, Executive Director

Mary Pickford Foundation
9171 Wilshire Boulevard
Suite 512
Beverly, Hills, CA 90210
(310) 273-2770

Description: Funds "well-established medical or community service organizations"
$ Given: 93 grants totaling $563,910; range, $135-$70,000
Application: Initial approach by letter
Deadline: None
Contact: Edward C. Stotsenberg, President

Santa Barbara Foundation
15 East Carillo Street
Santa Barbara, CA 93101
(805) 963-1873

Description: Funding includes social services, youth and health services
$ Given: 137 grants totaling $1,692,087
Application: N/A
Deadline: N/A
Contact: Edward R. Spaulding, Executive Director

The Sierra Foundation
12111 Gold Country Boulevard
Suite 101
Rancho Cordova, CA 95670
(916) 635-4745

Description: Funds health-related programs that will have a long-term impact on the general health of the population, will provide a positive change in health care systems or in the use of health care resources
$ Given: 64 grants totaling $1,592,162; average range, $20,000-$40,000
Application: Initial approach by letter
Deadline: None
Contact: Len McCandliss, President

Swig Foundation
c/o The Swig Foundations
Fairmont Hotel
San Francisco, CA 94016
(415) 772-5375

Description: Funding for arts, culture, education, community welfare, medical care, and projects in Israel
$ Given: 197 grants totaling $1,230,960; average range, $1,000-$65,000
Application: Initial approach by letter
Deadline: None
Contact: Nat Starr, Director

Sally B. Thornton Foundation
2125 Evergreen Street
San Diego, CA 92106

Description: Funds cultural programs, education, and health services
$ Given: 66 grants totaling $432,684; range, $10-$190,000
Application: Applications not accepted; giving to pre-selected organizations
Deadline: N/A
Contact: N/A

Van Nuys (I.N. and Susanna H.) Foundation
c/o Security Pacific
National Bank
P.O. Box 3189
Terminal Annex
Los Angeles, CA 90051

Description: Grants for health services and education
$ Given: 17 grants totaling $633,827; range, $4,000-$333,200
Application: Initial approach by letter
Deadline: None
Contact: Lorraine Tessier, Accountant

Van Nuys (J.B. and Emily) Charities
1800 Avenue of the Stars
Suite 345
Los Angeles, CA 90067
(213) 552-0175

Description: Funds hospitals and health service agencies, as well as child welfare and youth agencies
$ Given: 130 grants totaling $643,245; average, $5,000
Application: Proposal
Deadline: None
Contact: Robert Gibson Johnson, President

. . . .

**Wood-Claeyssens
Foundation**
P.O. Box 30547
Santa Barbara, CA 93130
(805) 682-4775

Description: Funds hospitals, health services, social services, and youth agencies
$ Given: 52 grants totaling $298,000; range, $500-$50,000
Application: Initial approach by letter
Deadline: August 31
Contact: Pierre V. Claeyssens, First Vice President

COLORADO

**The Anschutz Family
Foundation**
2400 Anaconda Tower
555 17th Street
Denver, CO 80202
(303) 293-2338

Description: Funds direct human services, especially for children, the elderly, and the poor, including health services
$ Given: 140 grants totaling $606,900; range, $100-$55,000
Application: Initial approach by letter
Deadline: March 1, September 1
Contact: Sue Anschutz Rodgers, President

**Comprecare Foundation,
Inc.**
P.O. Box 44170
Aurora, CO 80044
(303) 322-1641

Description: "To encourage, aid or assist specific health related programs and to support the activities of organizations and individuals who advance and promote health care education, the delivery of health care services, and the improvement of community health and welfare"
$ Given: 16 grants totaling $215,066; range, $2,000-$46,000
Application: Initial approach by letter
Deadline: None
Contact: N/A

Gates Foundation
3200 Cherry Creek So. Dr.
Suite 630
Denver, CO 80209
(303) 722-1881

Description: Funding interests include health care, health care cost reduction, and human services
$ Given: Grants totaling $3,911,887; high, $650,000
Application: Initial approach by telephone
Deadlines: January 15, April 15, July 15, and October 15
Contact: F. Charles Froelicher, Executive Director

• • • • • • • • • • • • • • • • • • • •

Johnson (Helen K. and Arthur E.) Foundation
1700 Broadway
Room 2302
Denver, CO 80290
(303) 861-4127

Description: "To solve human problems and enrich the quality of human life"
$ Given: 111 grants totaling $2,897,029; range, $100-$250,000
Application: Initial approach by letter or proposal
Deadline: January 1, April 1, July 1, and September 1
Contact: Stan Kamprath, Executive Director

Keebler Company Foundation
One Hollow Tree Lane
Elmhurst, Illinois 60126
(312) 833-2900

Description: Funding interests include minority programs, health and human services, and education
$ Given: 239 grants totaling $359,987; range, $10-$34,180
Areas of Support: Illinois, Colorado, Indiana, Maine, Minnesota, North Carolina, Pennsylvania, Texas
Application: Initial approach by letter
Deadline: None
Contact: A.G. Bland, Treasurer

Stern-Elder Memorial Trust
1700 Broadway
Denver, CO 80274

Description: Funds performing arts, health organizations, and social services
$ Given: 52 grants totaling $271,250; range, $100-$50,000
Application: N/A
Deadline: N/A
Contact: N/A

CONNECTICUT

Louis H. Aborn Foundation, Inc.
46 Wilshire Road
Greenwich, CT 06830
(203) 661-4046

Description: Funds public health projects, education, and child welfare
$ Given: Four grants totaling $151,000; range, $1,000-$90,000
Application: Initial approach by letter
Deadline: None
Contact: Louis H. Aborn, President

FLOW-THROUGH FUNDING

• • • • • • • • • • • • • • • • • • • •

Carolyn Foundation
1800 TCF Tower
Minneapolis, Minnesota
55402
(612) 339-7101

Description: Funding for health and welfare, education, culture, women, the environment, and the disadvantaged
$ Given: 37 grants totaling $989,665; range, $1,300-$100,000
Areas of Support: Minneapolis-St. Paul, Minnesota and New Haven, Connecticut
Application: Initial approach by letter
Deadline: January and February for grants under $10,000; January through July for grants over $10,000
Contact: Carol J. Fetzer, Executive Director

Crestlea Foundation, Inc.
1004 Wilmington Trust
Court
Wilmington, DE 19801

Description: Funding emphasis includes health agencies, higher and secondary education, social services, and youth agencies
$ Given: 35 grants totaling $527,765; range, $500-$225,565
Areas of Support: Delaware and Connecticut
Application: Initial approach by letter
Deadline: None
Contact: Stewart E. Poole, President

**Fairfield County
Cooperative Foundation**
Five Landmark Square
Stamford, CT 06901
(203) 323-7410

Description: Funds health and social services, arts and culture, and education
$ Given: 60 grants totaling $989,937; range, $1,000-$90,000
Application: Initial approach by letter requesting guidelines
Deadlines: One month prior to board meetings (board meets the third Friday in February, April, August, and October)
Contact: Betsy Rich, Executive Director

Fisher Foundation, Inc.
36 Brookside Boulevard
West Hartford, CT 06107
(203) 523-7247

Description: Funds a Jewish welfare federation, health services, education, housing, the disadvantaged, and the aged
$ Given: 69 grants totaling $435,543; range, $100-$69,000
Application: Initial approach by letter
Deadlines: February 1, May 1, October 1
Contact: N/A

Hagedorn Fund
c/o Manufacturers Hanover
Trust Company
270 Park Avenue
New York, NY 10017
(212) 270-9107

Description: Funding for education, hospitals and health agencies, the aged, youth agencies, medical research, community funds, and cultural organizations
$ Given: 114 grants totaling $1,110,000; range, $1,000-$85,000
Areas of Support: New York metropolitan area (including New Jersey and Connecticut)
Application: Proposal
Deadline: November 15
Contact: Robert Rosenthal, Vice President, Manufacturers Hanover Trust Company

Heublein Foundation, Inc.
P.O. Box 388
Farmington, CT 06032
(203) 677-4061

Description: Funding interests include hospitals and health services
$ Given: 89 grants totaling $827,478; range, $500-$126,000
Application: Initial approach by letter
Deadline: N/A
Contact: L. Eileen Hall, Treasurer

The Howard and Bush Foundation, Inc.
85 Gillett Street
Hartford, CT 06105
(203) 236-8595

Description: Funding emphasis includes health services
$ Given: 77 grants totaling $1,346,985; range, $3,500-$72,052
Areas of Support: Hartford, Connecticut and Troy, New York
Application: Initial approach by letter
Deadline: February 1, June 1, October 1
Contact: Nancy Roberts

The Travelers Companies Foundation
One Tower Square
Hanford, CT 06183
(203) 277-2307

Description: Funding interests include programs that benefit older Americans, and health and social services
$ Given: 171 grants totaling $4,043,833; range, $500-$835,000
Application: Proposal
Deadline: None
Contact: Janet C. French, Executive Director

FLOW-THROUGH FUNDING

• • • • • • • • • • • • • • • • • • •

The Waterbury Foundation
P.O. Box 252
Waterbury, CT 06720
(203) 753-1315

Description: Funds social services, health care, education, community funds, and the arts
$ Given: 45 grants totaling $269,946; range, $45-$100,000
Application: Initial approach by letter
Deadline: None
Contact: N/A

DELAWARE

Birch (Stephen and Mary) Foundation, Inc.
501 Silverside Road
Suite 13
Wilmington, DE 19809

Description: Funding emphasis includes health agencies, hospitals, social services, and youth agencies
$ Given: Eight grants totaling $1,695,500; range, $500-$1,500,000
Application: Initial approach by letter
Deadline: None
Contact: Elfriede Looze

Crestlea Foundation, Inc.
1004 Wilmington Trust
Court
Wilmington, DE 19801

Description: Funding emphasis includes health agencies, higher and secondary education, social services, and youth agencies
$ Given: 35 grants totaling $527,765; range, $500-$225,565
Application: Initial approach by letter
Deadline: None
Contact: Stewart E. Poole, President

Ederic Foundation, Inc.
Building C, Suite 300
3801 Kennett Pike
Greenville, DE 19807
(302) 654-9933

Description: Funding interests include hospitals and health care
$ Given: 94 grants totaling $329,805; range, $50-$38,000
Application: Initial approach by letter
Deadline: None
Contact: Harry S. Short, Secretary

• • • • • • • • • • • • • • • • • • •

DISTRICT OF COLUMBIA

Bender Foundation, Inc.
1120 Connecticut Avenue
NW
Suite 1200
Washington, DC 20036
(202) 828-9000

Description: Funding interests include education, health services, social welfare, Jewish organizations and welfare funds
$ Given: 65 grants totaling $395,200; range, $1,000-$100,000
Areas of Support: Washington, DC, and Maryland
Application: Initial approach by letter
Deadline: November 20
Contact: Sondra D. Bender, President

Fannie Mae Foundation
3900 Wisconsin Avenue,
N.W.
Washington, DC 20016
(202) 752-6500

Description: Funding interests include housing and community development, and health and social concerns
$ Given: 300 grants totaling $1,151,567; range, $100-$50,000
Areas of Support: Washington, DC; Pasadena, California; Atlanta, Georgia; Chicago, Illinois; and Philadelphia, Pennsylvania
Application: Proposal
Deadline: None
Contact: Harriet M. Ivey, Executive Director

The Favrot Fund
909 Wirt Road
No. 101
Houston, TX 77024
(713) 956-4009

Description: Focus on community-based programs directed toward health, the needy, and the arts
$ Given: 24 grants totaling $310,000; range, $2,000-$25,000
Areas of Support: Texas, California, New York, and Washington, DC
Application: Initial approach by letter
Deadline: None
Contact: Mrs. Carol Parker

. . . .

FLORIDA

John Blair Foundation
c/o Northern Trust Bank of
Florida/Naples, N.A.
530 Fifth Avenue So.
Naples, FL 33940
(813) 262-8800

Description: Funds health and social services, and family planning
$ Given: 48 grants totaling $105,600; range, $150-$15,000
Application: Application form not required
Deadline: None
Contact: N/A

Edyth Bush Charitable Foundation, Inc.
199 E. Wellbourne Ave.
P.O. Box 1967
Winter Park, FL 32790
(407) 647-4322

Description: Funds charitable, educational, and health service organizations, with emphasis on human services and health
$ Given: 58 grants totaling $2,260,296; range, $4,000-$170,000
Application: Initial approach by letter or proposal
Deadlines: September 1, January 1
Contact: H. Clifford Lee, President

Conn Memorial Foundation, Inc.
220 East Madison St.
Suite 822
P.O. Box 229
Tampa, FL 33601
(813) 223-3838

Description: Funds health services and rehabilitation and charities benefitting youth
$ Given: 49 grants totaling $778,220; range, $1,000-$175,000
Application: Initial approach by letter or proposal
Deadline: November 30, May 31
Contact: David B. Frye, President

Dade Community Foundation
200 South Biscayne Blvd.
Suite 4970
Miami, FL 33131
(305) 371-2711

Description: Funding interests include health, social services, the homeless and housing, education, arts and culture
$ Given: 305 grants totaling $1,601,360; range, $100-$62,140
Application: Initial approach by letter
Deadline: December 1
Contact: Ruth Shack, President

• • • • • • • • • • • • • • • • • •

James E. Davis Family -
W.D. Charities
5050 Edgewood Court
Jacksonville, FL 32205

Description: Areas of support include education, medical research, and health services
$ Given: 19 grants totaling $130,650; range, $100-$50,000
Application: N/A
Deadline:N/A
Contact: N/A

Tine W. Davis Family -
W.D. Charities, Inc.
4190 Belfort Road
Suite 240
Jacksonville, FL 32216

Description: Areas of support include education, health and social service agencies, and medical research
$ Given: 117 grants totaling $762,425; range, $10,000-$100,000
Application: Initial approach by letter
Deadline: None
Contact: Charitable Grants Commission

Jefferson Lee Ford III
Memorial Foundation, Inc.
c/o Sun Bank Miami
9600 Collins Avenue
P.O. Box 546487
Bal Harbour, FL 33154
(305) 868-2630

Description: Funds health agencies, education, and medical research
$ Given: 48 grants totaling $198,500; range, $1,000-$15,000
Application: Initial approach by letter
Deadline: None
Contact: Herbert L. Kurras, Sr., Director

Charles A. Frueauff
Foundation
306 East Seventh Ave.
Tallahassee, FL 32303
(904) 561-3508

Description: Areas of support include hospitals, mental health and other health services
$ Given: 195 grants totaling $2,824,500; range, $1,500-$50,000
Application: Initial approach by letter, telephone, or proposal
Deadline: March 15
Contact: David A. Frueauff, Secretary

• • • • • • • • • • • • • • • • • • •

K.W. Grader Foundation, Inc.
1925 Hermosa Street
Bartow, FL 33830
(813) 533-1048

Description: Funding for health services, higher education, religious giving, and social services, including child welfare
$ Given: 67 grants totaling $292,990; range, $250-$25,000
Application: Applications not accepted; giving to pre-selected organizations
Deadline: N/A
Contact: E.L. Grader, Vice President

Lost Tree Charitable Foundation, Inc.
11555 Lost Tree Way
North Palm Beach, FL 33408
(407) 622-3780

Description: Funding interests include education and health services
$ Given: 30 grants totaling $146,354; range, $500-$14,500
Application: Initial approach by letter
Deadline: None
Contact: Pamela M. Rue. Executive Secretary

D.W. McMillan Foundation
329 Belleville Avenue
P.O. Box 867
Brewton, AL 36427
(205) 867-4881

Description: Funds local health and welfare organizations (limited to programs giving direct aid)
$ Given: 21 grants totaling $392,000; range, $1,500-$60,000
Areas of Support: Escambia County, Alabama, and Escambia County, Florida
Application: Initial approach by letter
Deadline: December 1
Contact: James D. Nabors, Secretary-Treasurer

Monsanto Fund
800 North Lindbergh Blvd.
St. Louis, MO 63167
(314) 694-4596

Description: Funding interests include health services, hospitals, social services, youth, education (science and mathematics), and community funds
$ Given: Grants totaling $8,285,748; range, $100-$1,112,000
Areas of Support: Alabama, California, Florida, Georgia, Idaho, Illinois, Massachusetts, Maine, Missouri, New Jersey, North Carolina, Ohio, South Carolina, Texas, and West Virginia
Application: Proposal
Deadline: None
Contact: John L. Mason, President

· · · · · · · · · · · · · · · · · · · ·

Martha G. Moore Foundation, Inc.
850 S.E. 7th Street
Suite A
Deerfield Beach, FL 33441

Description: Funds health and social services
$ Given: 13 grants totaling $125,000; range, $2,000-$28,000
Application: N/A
Deadline: N/A
Contact: N/A

The Retirement Research Foundation
1300 West Higgins Road
Suite 214
Park Ridge, IL 60068
(708) 823-4133

Description: Focus is the improvement of the quality of life of older persons in the United States.
$ Given: Grants totaling $4,131,981; average, $25,000
Areas of Support: Florida, Illinois, Indiana, Iowa, Kentucky, Missouri, and Wisconsin
Application: Initial approach by letter
Deadlines: February 1, May 1, and August 1
Contact: Marilyn Hennessy, Senior Vice President

Wilson (Hugh and Mary) Foundation, Inc.
c/o Wood and Seitl
240 North Washington Blvd.
Suite 460
Sarasota, FL 34236
(813) 954-2155

Description: Areas of support include cancer research and health services, the performing arts, and social service issues
$ Given: 26 grants totaling $238,291; range, $1,000-$50,000
Areas of Support: Manatee-Sarasota, Florida; Lewisburg-Danville, Pennsylvania
Application: Initial approach by letter
Deadline: None
Contact: John R. Wood, President

GEORGIA

Allen Foundation, Inc.
Box 1712
Atlanta, GA 30301
(404) 332-3000

Description: Funds education, health services, and cultural programs
$ Given: 73 grants totaling $289,066; range, $100-$47,400
Application: Application form required
Deadline: June 30
Contact: Roger E. Herndon, Secretary-Treasurer

FLOW-THROUGH FUNDING

· ·

Fannie Mae Foundation
3900 Wisconsin Ave., NW
Washington, DC 20016
(202) 752-6500

Description: Funding interests include housing and community development, and health and social concerns
$ Given: 300 grants totaling $1,151,567; range, $100-$50,000
Areas of Support: Washington, DC; Pasadena, California; Atlanta, Georgia; Chicago, Illinois; and Philadelphia, Pennsylvania
Application: Proposal
Deadline: None
Contact: Harriet M. Ivey, Executive Director

**Fort Howard
Foundation, Inc.**
P.O. Box 11325
Green Bay, WI 54307
(414) 435-8821

Description: Areas of support include education, health care facilities, cultural programs, and social service and youth agencies
$ Given: 6 grants totaling $726,652; range, $13,700-$150,000
Areas of Support: Green Bay, Wisconsin; Muskogee, Oklahoma; and Effingham County, Georgia
Application: The foundation is not presently making any new funding commitments
Contact: Bruce W. Nagel, Executive Director

**The Lee (Ray M. & Mary
Elizabeth) Foundation, Inc.**
c/o Citizens and Southern
Trust Co.
P.O. Box 4446
Atlanta, GA 30302
(404) 897-3222

Description: Areas of support include health agencies, educational institutions, hospitals, religious organizations and the arts.
$ Given: 62 grants totaling $360,000; range, $1,000-$25,000
Application: Proposal
Deadlines: January 31, April 30, July 31, and October 31
Contact: Larry B. Hooks, Administrative Manager

· · · · · · · · · · · · · · · · · ·

Monsanto Fund
800 North Lindbergh Blvd.
St. Louis, MO 63167
(314) 694-4596

Description: Funding interests include health services, hospitals, social services, youth, education (science and mathematics), and community funds
$ Given: Grants totaling $8,285,748; range, $100-$1,112,000
Areas of Support: Alabama, California, Florida, Georgia, Idaho, Illinois, Massachusetts, Maine, Missouri, New Jersey, North Carolina, Ohio, South Carolina, Texas, and West Virginia
Application: Proposal
Deadline: None
Contact: John L. Mason, President

HAWAII

First Hawaiian Foundation
165 South King Street
Honolulu, HI 96813
(808) 525-8144

Description: Funds social services, health services, education, and a church and community fund
$ Given: 50 grants totaling $733,536; range, $177-$127,000
Application: Initial approach by letter
Deadline: None
Contact: Herbert E. Wolff, Secretary

Hawaiian Electric Industries Charitable Foundation
P.O. Box 730
Honolulu, HI 96808
(808) 543-7356

Description: Funding interests include health, hospitals, and community development
$ Given: 201 grants totaling $812,000; range, $300-$25,000
Application: Initial approach by letter with project data
Deadline: December 1, June 1
Contact: Ted Souza

IDAHO

George Frederick Jewett Foundation
One Maritime Plaza
Suite 990
San Franciso, CA 94111
(415) 421-1351

Description: Interests include health care and medical research and services
$ Given: 134 grants totaling $953,597; range, $500-$25,000
Areas of Support: San Francisco, California; eastern Washington; northern Idaho
Application: Initial approach by letter
Deadlines: February 15, May 15, August 15, and November 1
Contact: Theresa A. Mullen, Program Director

FLOW-THROUGH FUNDING

• • • • • • • • • • • • • • • • • • •

Meyer Memorial Trust
1515 S.W. Fifth Avenue
Suite 500
Portland, OR 97201
(503) 228-5512

Description: General purpose grants in Oregon for education, health and social welfare, arts and humanities; special program grants for Aging and Independence and Support for Children at Risk in Oregon, Alaska, Idaho, Montana, and Washington; operates a Small Grants Program (500-$8,000) for small projects in Oregon
$ Given: 209 grants totaling $11,953,746; range, $500-$2,000,000
Application: Application form required
Deadline: April 1, October 1 for Aging and Independence; July 15, October 15 for Small Grants Program; no deadline for general purpose grants
Contact: Charles S. Rooks, Executive Director

Monsanto Fund
800 North Lindbergh Blvd.
St. Louis, MO 63167
(314) 694-4596

Description: Funding interests include health services, hospitals, social services, youth, education (science and mathematics), and community funds
$ Given: Grants totaling $8,285,748; range, $100-$1,112,000
Areas of Support: Alabama, California, Florida, Georgia, Idaho, Illinois, Massachusetts, Maine, Missouri, New Jersey, North Carolina, Ohio, South Carolina, Texas, and West Virginia
Application: Proposal
Deadline: None
Contact: John L. Mason, President

Spokane Inland Northwest Community Foundation
400 Paulsen Center
West 421 Riverside Ave.
Spokane, Washington 99201
(509) 624-2606

Description: Funding interests include the elderly, music and the arts, social and health services, and education
$ Given: 440 grants totaling $738,429; average grant, $1,500
Areas of Support: The inland northwest (Washington and Idaho)
Application: Initial approach by letter
Deadlines: October 1 (Spokane, Washington); November 1 (Pullman and Dayton, Washington); May 1 (northern Idaho); and October 15 (ISC fund)
Contact: Jeanne L. Ager, Executive Director

ILLINOIS

The Blum (Nathan and Emily S.) Fund
c/o Harris Bank
111 West Monroe Street
P.O. Box 755
Chicago, IL 60690
(312) 461-2613

Description: Funds hospitals, health and social service agencies (including Jewish welfare funds)
$ Given: 10 grants totaling $360,000; range, $2,000-$102,000
Application: Proposal
Deadline: None
Contact: Ellen A. Bechtold, Vice President, Harris Trust and Savings Bank

Blum-Kovler Foundation
500 North Michigan Avenue
Chicago, IL 60611
(312) 828-9777

Description: Areas of support include education, hospitals, health services, and medical research
$ Given: 148 grants totaling $1,360,850; range, $500-$310,000
Application: Initial approach by letter
Deadline: None
Contact: H. Jonathan Kovler, Treasurer

Borg-Warner Foundation, Inc.
200 South Michigan Avenue
Chicago, IL 60604
(312) 322-8659

Description: Funding interests include community funds, social welfare, and health services
$ Given: 150 grants totaling $1,295,445; range, $500-$200,000
Aplication: Initial approach by letter of intent
Deadline: March 1 (letter of intent); May 1 (proposal)
Contact: Ellen J. Benjamin, Director of Corporate Contributions

Fred J. Brunner Foundation
9300 King Street
Franklin Park, IL 60131

Description: Funds education, and social, health, and youth services.
$ Given: Grants totaling $221,540; range, $100-$20,000
Application: Proposal
Deadline: December 15
Contact: A.J. Schwegel, Vice President

FLOW-THROUGH FUNDING

• • • • • • • • • • • • • • • • • • • •

A. C. Bueler
Foundation
c/o Continental Illinois
National Bank and Trust
Colorado. of Chicago
30 North LaSalle St.
Chicago, IL 60693
(312) 828-1785

Description: Funds hospitals, health services, medical research, and education
$ Given: Five grants totaling $431,000
Application: Initial approach by letter
Deadline: None
Contact: M.C. Ryan

John Deere Foundation
John Deere Road
Moline, IL 61265
(309) 765-4137

Description: Areas of support include health services, community funds, youth agencies, and education
$ Given: Grants totaling $3,707,974; range, $300-$539,000
Areas of Support: Iowa, Illinois, Wisconsin
Application: Initial approach by letter
Deadline: None
Contact: Donald R. Morgenthaler, President

The Donaldson
Foundation
c/o Donaldson Company,
Inc.
P.O. Box 1299
Minneapolis, MN 55440
(612) 887-3010

Description: Funding interests include health services, environmental protection, and higher education
$ Given: 98 grants totaling $338,875; range, $300-$38,400
Areas of Support: Illinois, Indiana, Iowa, Kentucky, Minnesota, Missouri, and Wisconsin
Application: Initial approach by letter
Deadline: May 1, August 1
Contact: Raymond Vodovnik, Secretary

The Dumke (Dr. Ezekial
R. and Edna Wattis)
Foundation
600 Crandall Building
10 West First South
Salt Lake City, UT 84101
(801) 363-7863

Description: Funds education, medical and hospital services, youth agencies, and cultural programs
$ Given: 27 grants totaling $262,113; range, $1,000-$40,000
Areas of Support: Utah and Illinois
Application: Application form required
Deadline: February 1, July 1
Contact: Max B. Lewis, Secretary

• • • • • • • • • • • • • • • • • •

Fannie Mae Foundation
3900 Wisconsin Avenue NW
Washington, DC 20016
(202) 752-6500

Description: Funding interests include housing and community development, and health and social concerns
$ Given: 300 grants totaling $1,151,567; range, $100-$50,000
Areas of Support: Washington, DC; Pasadena, California; Atlanta, Georgia; Chicago, Illinois; and Philadelphia, Pennsylvania
Application: Proposal
Deadline: None
Contact: Harriet M. Ivey, Executive Director

The Field Foundation of Illinois, Inc.
135 South LaSalle Street
Chicago, Il 60603
(312) 263-3211

Description: Funds health, community welfare, education, and cultural activities
$ Given: 57 grants totaling $1,579,109; range, $5,000-$97,000
Application: Proposal
Deadline: None
Contact: Handy L. Lindsey, Jr., Executive Director

Lloyd A. Fry Foundation
135 South LaSalle Street
Suite 1910
Chicago, IL 60603
(312) 580-0310

Description: Areas of support include education, public policy, health and social services
$ Given: 153 grants totaling $2,651,460; range, $1,000-$115,000
Application: Initial approach by letter
Deadline: None
Contact: Ben Rothblatt, Executive Director

Iowa and Illinois Gas and Electric Company Giving Program
206 East Second Street
Davenport, IA 52802
(319) 326-7038

Description: Areas of support include education, health care, child welfare, civic affairs, community development, and family services
$ Given: 186 grants totaling $ 537,065; range, $10-$106,375
Areas of Support: Davenport, Bettendorf, Cedar Rapids, Iowa City, and Fort Dodge, Iowa; Rock Island and Moline, Illinois; and Ohio
Application: Initial approach by letter
Deadline: None
Contact: J.C. Decker, Secretary-Treasurer

. . . .

Keebler Company
Foundation
One Hollow Tree Lane
Elmhurst, IL 60126
(312) 833-2900

Description: Funding interests include minority programs, health and human services, and education
$ Given: 239 grants totaling $359,987; range, $10-$34,180
Areas of Support: Illinois, Colorado, Indiana, Maine, Minnesota, North Carolina, Pennsylvania, Texas
Application: Initial approach by letter
Deadline: None
Contact: A.G. Bland, Treasurer

Material Service
Foundation
222 North LaSalle Street
Chicago, IL 60675

Description: Funding interests include health services, education, cultural activities, and community development
$ Given: 139 grants totaling $283,100; range, $25-$100,000
Application: Initial approach by letter
Deadline: None
Contact: Louis J. Levy, Administrator

Monsanto Fund
800 North Lindbergh Blvd.
St. Louis, MO 63167
(314) 694-4596

Description: Funding interests include health services, hospitals, social services, youth, education (science and mathematics), and community funds
$ Given: Grants totaling $8,285,748; range, $100-$1,112,000
Areas of Support: Alabama, California, Florida, Georgia, Idaho, Illinois, Massachusetts, Maine, Missouri, New Jersey, North Carolina, Ohio, South Carolina, Texas, and West Virginia
Application: Proposal
Deadline: None
Contact: John L. Mason, President

Morton International
Foundation
110 North Wacker Dr.
Chicago, IL 60606

Description: Funds health and social services, education, civic affairs, and cultural programs
Given: 96 grants totaling $390,614; range, $500-$121,700
Application: Initial approach by letter
Deadline: None
Contact: N/A

The Northern Trust Company Charitable Trust
c/o The Northern Trust Company
50 South LaSalle Street
Chicago, IL 60675
(312) 444-3538

Description: Funds community development, health services, education, and social service
$ Given: 645 grants totaling $1,182,538; range, $25-$154,000
Application: Initial approach by letter or brief proposal
Deadline: Health: February 1
Contact: Marjorie W. Lundy, Vice President

The Retirement Research Foundation
1300 West Higgins Road
Suite 214
Park Ridge, IL 60068
(708) 823-4133

Description: Focus is the improvement of the quality of life of older persons in the United States.
$ Given: Grants totaling $4,131,981; average, $25,000
Areas of Support: Florida, Illinois, Indiana, Iowa, Kentucky, Missouri, and Wisconsin
Application: Initial approach by letter
Deadlines: February 1, May 1, and August 1
Contact: Marilyn Hennessy, Senior Vice President

Rothschild (Hulda B. and Maurice L.) Foundation
c/o First National Bank of Chicago
One First National Plaza
Suite 0101
Chicago, IL 60603
(312) 732-6473

Description: "Giving primarily toward improving the quality of life for older adults in the U.S.; the foundation is particularly interested in innovative projects which develop and/or demonstrate new approaches to the problems of older adults and which have the potential for significant impact"
$ Given: 14 grants totaling $523,485; range, $550-$523,585 **Application:** Initial approach by letter
Deadline: None
Contact: Donald A. Kress

The Otto S. A. Sprague Memorial Institute
c/o Harris Trust and Savings Bank
190 South LaSalle Street
Fourth Floor
Chicago, IL 60690
(312) 461-7054

Description: Funding interests include the prevention and relief of human suffering caused by disease.
$ Given: Five grants totaling $600,000; range, $15,000-$190,000
Application: Initial approach by letter
Deadline: None
Contact: Thomas E. Macior

FLOW-THROUGH FUNDING

• • • • • • • • • • • • • • • • • • • •

Sundstrand Corporation Foundation
4949 Harrison Avenue
P.O. Box 7003
Rockford, IL 61125
(815) 226-6000

Description: Areas of support include community funds, education, social and health services
$ Given: 112 grants totaling $845,850; range, $450-$122,000
Application: Initial approach by letter
Deadline: None
Contact: Clarence Kieselburg, Secretary

Washington Square Health Foundation
875 North Michigan Avenue
Suite 3516
Chicago, IL 60611
(312) 664-6488

Description: Funds health services, medical research, and medical education
$ Given: 36 grants totaling $812,993; range, $1,000-$200,000
Application: Application form required
Deadline: June 1, December 1
Contact: Howard Nochumson, Executive Director

INDIANA

The Donaldson Foundation
c/o Donaldson Company, Inc.
P.O. Box 1299
Minneapolis, MN 55440
(612) 887-3010

Description: Funding interests include health services, environmental protection, and higher education
$ Given: 98 grants totaling $338,875; range, $300-$38,400
Areas of Support: Illinois, Indiana, Iowa, Kentucky, Minnesota, Missouri, and Wisconsin
Application: Initial approach by letter
Deadline: May 1, August 1
Contact: Raymond Vodovnik, Secretary

Fort Wayne Community Foundation
116 East Wayne Street
Fort Wayne, IN 46802
(219) 426-4083

Description: Areas of support include health services, social services, education, community development, and the arts
$ Given: 62 grants totaling $295,837; range, $65-$18,000
Application: Initial approach by letter, proposal, or telephone
Deadline: None
Contact: Mrs. Barbara Burt, Executive Director

• • • • • • • • • • • • • • • • • • • •

**The Indianapolis
Foundation**
615 North Alabama Street
Room 119
Indianapolis, IN 46204
(317) 634-7497

Description: Areas of support include health, welfare, and education
$ Given: 84 grants totaling $2,967,065; average range, $4,000-$50,000
Application: Initial approach by letter or telephone
Deadlines: Last day of January, March, May, July, September, or November
Contact: Kenneth I. Chapman, Executive Director

**Keebler Company
Foundation**
One Hollow Tree Lane
Elmhurst, IL 60126
(312) 833-2900

Description: Funding interests include minority programs, health and human services, and education
$ Given: 239 grants totaling $359,987; range, $10-$34,180
Areas of Support: Illinois, Colorado, Indiana, Maine, Minnesota, North Carolina, Pennsylvania, Texas
Application: Initial approach by letter
Deadline: None
Contact: A.G. Bland, Treasurer

**E.H. Kilbourne Residuary
Charitable Trust**
c/o Lincoln National Bank
Trust Department
P.O. Box 9340
Fort Wayne, IN 46899
(219) 461-6451

Description: Funding interests include education, youth agencies, health and social services, and the arts
$ Given: 30 grants totaling $192,558; range, $200-$19,800
Application: Initial approach by letter
Deadline: None
Contact: Alice Kopfer, Vice President

Miles Foundation
1127 Myrtle Street
P.O. Box 40
Elkhart, IN 46515
(219) 264-8225

Description: Areas of support include community funds, education, hospitals and health organizations
Given: 113 grants totaling $511,023; range, $100-$50,000
Application: Initial approach by letter
Deadline: None
Contact: Lehman H. Beardsley, Chairman

FLOW-THROUGH FUNDING

•   •

The Retirement Research Foundation
1300 West Higgins Rd.
Suite 214
Park Ridge, IL 60068
(708) 823-4133

Description: Focus is the improvement of the quality of life of older persons in the United States.
$ Given: Grants totaling $4,131,981; **average,** $25,000
Areas of Support: Florida, Illinois, Indiana, Iowa, Kentucky, Missouri, and Wisconsin
Application: Initial approach by letter
Deadlines: February 1, May 1, and August 1
Contact: Marilyn Hennessy, Senior Vice President

IOWA

John Deere Foundation
John Deere Road
Moline, IL 61265
(309) 765-4137

Description: Areas of support include health services, community funds, youth agencies, and education
$ Given: Grants totaling $3,707,974; range, $300-$539,000
Areas of Support: Iowa, Illinois, Wisconsin
Application: Initial approach by letter
Deadline: None
Contact: Donald R. Morgenthaler, President

The Donaldson Foundation
c/o Donaldson Company, Inc.
P.O. Box 1299
Minneapolis, MN 55440
(612) 887-3010

Description: Funding interests include health services, environmental protection, and higher education
$ Given: 98 grants totaling $338,875; range, $300-$38,400
Areas of Support: Illinois, Indiana, Iowa, Kentucky, Minnesota, Missouri, and Wisconsin
Application: Initial approach by letter
Deadline: May 1, August 1
Contact: Raymond Vodovnik, Secretary

The Hall Foundation, Inc.
115 Third Street SE
No. 803
Cedar Rapids, IA 52401
(319) 362-90779

Description: Funds cultural programs, a community fund, hospitals, and health services
$ Given: 35 grants totaling $3,395,564; range, $500-$680,000
Application: Initial approach by letter
Deadline: None
Contact: John G. Lidvall, Executive Director

• • • • • • • • • • • • • • • • • • •

Iowa and Illinois Gas and Electric Company Giving Program
206 East Second Street
Davenport, IA 52802
(319) 326-7038

Description: Areas of support include education, health care, child welfare, civic affairs, community development, and family services
$ Given: 186 grants totaling $ 537,065; range, $10-$106,375
Areas of Support: Davenport, Bettendorf, Cedar Rapids, Iowa City, and Fort Dodge, Iowa; Rock Island and Moline, Illinois; and Ohio
Application: Initial approach by letter
Deadline: None
Contact: J.C. Decker, Secretary-Treasurer

Mid-Iowa Health Foundation
550 39th Street
Suite 104
Des Moines, IA 50312
(515) 277-6411

Description: Funds health-related service projects (including drug abuse, mental health, and nutrution)
$ Given: 41 grants totaling $459,129; range, $700-$27,345
Application: Initial approach by letter
Deadline: February 1, May 1, August 1, and November 1
Contact: Kathryn Bradley

The Retirement Research Foundation
1300 West Higgins Road
Suite 214
Park Ridge, IL 60068
(708) 823-4133

Description: Focus is the improvement of the quality of life of older persons in the United States.
$ Given: Grants totaling $4,131,981; **average,** $25,000
Areas of Support: Florida, Illinois, Indiana, Iowa, Kentucky, Missouri, and Wisconsin
Application: Initial approach by letter
Deadlines: February 1, May 1, and August 1
Contact: Marilyn Hennessy, Senior Vice President

KANSAS

Arkla Corporate Giving Program
400 East Capitol Avenue
P.O. Box 751
Little Rock, AK 72203
(501) 377-4610

Description: Funds a wide variety of programs, including health services, mental health, AIDS, child welfare and drug abuse.
$ Given: N/A
Limitations: Giving in major operating areas (Arkansas, California, Kansas, Texas, Oklahoma, and Mississippi)
Application: Initial approach by letter
Deadline: None
Contact: James L. Rutherford III, Senior Vice President (Little Rock, Arkansas area) or Hugh H. McCastlain (Shreveport, Louisiana area)

FLOW-THROUGH FUNDING

• • • • • • • • • • • • • • • • • • • •

Ewing Marion Kauffman Foundation
922 Walnut Street
Suite 1100
Kansas City, MO 64106
(816) 966-4000

Description: Funds health agencies, childhood education, and family services
$ Given: 20 grants totaling $201,639; range, $50-$75,000
Areas of Support: Kansas and Missouri
Application: Brief concept paper
Deadline: None
Contact: Carl Mitchell, Treasurer

Rice (Ethel and Raymond F.) Foundation
700 Massachusetts Street
Lawrence, Kansas 66044
(913) 843-0420

Description: Areas of support include education, health, youth and social service agencies
$ Given: 80 grants totaling $235,885; range, $500-$16,000
Application: Proposal
Deadline: November 15
Contact: George M. Klem, Treasurer

KENTUCKY

James Graham Brown Foundation, Inc.
132 East Gray Street
Louisville, KY 40202
(502) 583-4085

Description: Funding interests include community development, health services, and youth
$ Given: 60 grants totaling $8,459,687; range, $100-$1,500,000
Application: Initial approach by letter
Deadline: None
Contact: Mason Rummel, Grants Coordinator

The Cralle Foundation
c/o Liberty National Bank
and Trust Co. of Louisville
P.O. Box 32500
Louisville, KY 40232
(502) 566-1702

Description: Funds education, health services, youth groups, community development, and museums
$ Given: 18 grants totaling $785,833; range, $3,500-$300,000
Application: Application form required
Deadline: None
Contact: Institutional Trust Department

• • • • • • • • • • • • • • • • • • • •

The Donaldson Foundation
c/o Donaldson Company, Inc.
P.O. Box 1299
Minneapolis, MN 55440
(612) 887-3010

Description: Funding interests include health services, environmental protection, and higher education
$ Given: 98 grants totaling $338,875; range, $300-$38,400
Areas of Support: Illinois, Indiana, Iowa, Kentucky, Minnesota, Missouri, and Wisconsin
Application: Initial approach by letter
Deadline: May 1, August 1
Contact: Raymond Vodovnik, Secretary

Kentucky Fried Chicken Corporate Giving Program
P.O. Box 32070
Louisville, KY 40232
(502) 456-8300

Description: Funding interests include health services, arts, drug rehabilitation, education, and community development
$ Given: N/A
Application: N/A
Deadline:N/A
Contact: Gregg M. Reynolds, Vice President, Public Affairs

The Retirement Research Foundation
1300 West Higgins Road
Suite 214
Park Ridge, IL 60068
(708) 823-4133

Description: Focus is the improvement of the quality of life of older persons in the United States.
$ Given: Grants totaling $4,131,981; **average,** $25,000
Areas of Support: Florida, Illinois, Indiana, Iowa, Kentucky, Missouri, and Wisconsin
Application: Initial approach by letter
Deadlines: February 1, May 1, and August 1
Contact: Marilyn Hennessy, Senior Vice President

LOUISIANA

The Community Foundation of Shreveport-Bossier
401 Edwards Street
Suite 1520
Shreveport, LA 71101
(318) 221-0582

Description: Funds health services, education, youth agencies, welfare, and cultural programs
$ Given: 41 grants totaling $691,920; range, $170-$100,000
Application: Initial approach by letter
Deadline: March 1, June 1, September 1
Contact: Carol Emanuel, Executive Director

FLOW-THROUGH FUNDING

. . . .

German Protestant Orphan Asylum Association
5342 St. Charles Ave.
New Orleans, LA 70115
(504) 895-2361

Description: Areas of support include medical services, child welfare, family services, and, youth programs
$ Given: 18 grants totaling $227,194; range, $1,980-$35,931
Application: Initial approach by letter
Deadline: December, March, June, and September
Contact: Everett T. Aultman, Executive Director

Goldring Family Foundation
809 Jefferson Highway
Jefferson, LA 70121

Description: Funding interests include health services and community funds, with emphasis on Jewish welfare and education
$ Given: 29 grants totaling $384,640; range, $100-$200,000
Application: Application form not required
Deadline: None
Contact: N/A

MAINE

Agnes M. Lindsay Trust
45 Market Street
Manchester, NH 03101
(603) 669-4140

Description: Funding interests include health services, higher education, services for the handicapped, and welfare institutions
$ Given: 191 grants totaling $863,771; average range, $1,000-$10,000
Areas of Support: Maine, Massachusetts, New Hampshire, and Vermont
Application: Proposal
Deadline: None
Contact: Robert L. Chiesa, Trustee

UNUM Charitable Foundation
2211 Congress Street
Portland, ME 04122
(207) 770-2211

Description: 75% of annual funds go to corporate community grants for health and welfare agencies, arts and cultural programs, education, and civic organizations; 25% to AIDS and aging programs
$ Given: 157 grants totaling $813,833; range, $25-$208,865
Application: Initial approach by letter
Deadline: None
Contact: Judith Nedeau Harrison, Director, Corporate Public Involvement

• •

MARYLAND

The Abell Foundation
1116 Fidelity Building
210 North Charles Street
Baltimore, MD 21201
(301) 547-1300

Description: Funding interests include education, health and family services, arts and culture
$ Given: 188 grants totaling $ 5,650,687; average, $15,000
Application: Initial approach by letter
Deadline: January 1, March 1, May 1, July 1, September 1, November 1
Contact: Robert C. Embry, Jr., President

Bender Foundation, Inc.
1120 Connecticut Avenue, NW
Suite 1200
Washington, DC 20036
(202) 828-9000

Description: Funding interests include education, health services, social welfare, Jewish organizations and welfare funds
$ Given: 65 grants totaling $395,200; range, $1,000-$100,000
Areas of Support: Washington, DC, and Maryland
Application: Initial approach by letter
Deadline: November 20
Contact: Sondra D. Bender, President

The Blaustein (Louis and Henrietta) Foundation, Inc.
Blaustein Building
P.O. Box 238
Baltimore, MD 21203

Description: Funding interests include hospitals and health services, music and the arts, education, Jewish welfare funds, and a community fund
$ Given: 29 grants totaling $773,185; range, $500-$360,485
Application: Initial approach by letter
Deadline: None
Contact: Morton K. Blaustein, President

The Columbia Foundation
5430 Vantage Point Road
Columbia, MD 21044
(301) 730-7840

Description: Funding for health and human services, educational programs, housing, and arts and culture
$ Given: 40 grants totaling $382,000; range, $500-$20,000
Application: Initial approach by telephone
Deadline: January, September
Contact: Barbara K. Lawson, Executive Director

FLOW-THROUGH FUNDING

• • • • • • • • • • • • • • • • • • • •

The Ryland Group
Corporate Giving Program
10221 Wincopin Circle
P.O. Box 4000
Columbia, MD 21044
(301) 730-7222

Description: Funding interests include cancer, heart disease, and mental health, hunger, programs for the aged, child and family welfare, alcoholism and drug abuse
$ Given: 162 grants totaling $1,100,000; range, $100-$15,000
Application: Initial approach by letter
Deadline: None
Contact: Nancy L. Smith, Vice President, Public Affairs

Signet Bank/Maryland
Giving Program
Marketing-TU307
P.O. Box 1077
Baltimore, MD 21203
(301) 332-5000

Description: Funds arts and culture, civic affairs, education, and health
$ Given: Grants totaling $633,000
Application: N/A
Deadline: N/A
Contact: Corporate Contributions committee

MASSACHUSETTS

Boston Edison Foundation
800 Boylston Street
P359
Boston, MA 02199
(617) 424-2302

Description: Funds higher education, health and welfare organizations, community development, and arts and cultural programs
$ Given: 97 grants totaling $1,074,230; range, $500-$375,000
Application: Proposal, IRS 501C3 form, annual report, project budget, and contributors list
Deadline: November 1
Contact: Neil F. Doherty, Director

The Boston Globe Foundation II, Inc.
135 Morrissey Boulevard
Boston, MA 02107
(617) 929-3194

Description: Funding interests include education, community services, hospitals and health care, and the media business
$ Given: 499 grants totaling $4,284,715; range, $25-$340,000
Application: Proposal
Deadline: None
Contact: Suzanne Watkin, Executive Director

Donaldson (Oliver S. and Jennie R.) Charitable Trust
c/o Durfee Attleboro Bank, Trust Department
Ten North Main Street
Fall River, MA 02720
(617) 679-8311

Description: Areas of support include cancer research and treatment, hospitals and health agencies, education, and child welfare and youth agencies
$ Given: 37 grants totaling $858,440; range, $1,680-$68,000
Application: Application form required
Deadline: None
Contact: N/A

The Hopedale Foundation
43 Hope Street
Hopedale, MA 01747
(508) 473-0820

Description: Emphasis on area community funds, with support for hospitals, health services, youth agencies, and higher education
$ Given: 22 grants totaling $163,433; range, $1,500-$55,000
Application: Initial approach by letter
Deadline: None
Contact: Thad R. Jackson, Treasurer

Marion Gardner Jackson Charitable Trust
c/o The First National Bank of Boston
P.O. Box 1861
Boston, MA 02105
(617) 434-5669

Description: Capital funds for youth, health and services, and arts and cultural programs
$ Given: Grants totaling $239,500
Application: Proposal
Deadline: September 1
Contact: Sharon M. Driscoll, Trust Officer

FLOW-THROUGH FUNDING

· ·

Agnes M. Lindsay Trust
45 Market Street
Manchester,
New Hampshire 03101
(603) 669-4140

Description: Funding interests include health services, higher education, services for the handicapped, and welfare institutions
$ Given: 191 grants totaling $863,771; average range, $1,000-$10,000
Areas of Support: Maine, Massachusetts, New Hampshire, and Vermont
Application: Proposal
Deadline: None
Contact: Robert L. Chiesa, Trustee

Monsanto Fund
800 North Lindbergh Blvd.
St. Louis, MO 63167
(314) 694-4596

Description: Funding interests include health services, hospitals, social services, youth, education (science and mathematics), and community funds
$ Given: Grants totaling $8,285,748; range, $100-$1,112,000
Areas of Support: Alabama, California, Florida, Georgia, Idaho, Illinois, Massachusetts, Maine, Missouri, New Jersey,
North Carolina, Ohio, South Carolina, Texas, and West Virginia
Application: Proposal
Deadline: None
Contact: John L. Mason, President

Shawmut Worcester County Bank Charitable Foundation, Inc.
c/o Shawmut Central Tax Unit
446 Main Street
Worcester, MA 01608
(617) 793-4401

Description: Funding interests include education, health and social services, youth agencies, and cultural programs
$ Given: 52 grants totaling $301,350; range, $500-$75,000
Application: Initial approach by letter
Deadline: None
Contact: N/A

• • • • • • • • • • • • • • • • • • • •

TJX Foundation
c/o TJX Companies
770 Cochituale Road
Framingham, MA 01701
(508) 651-8714

Description: Funds health and social service programs emphasizing women, the elderly, the handicapped, minority groups, and the poor
$ Given: Grants totaling $1,269,975
Application: Proposal
Deadline: None
Contact: Rhonda Boccio

MICHIGAN

ANR Foundation, Inc.
One Woodward Avenue
Detroit, MI 48226
(313) 965-1200

Description: Funds health and welfare, education, culture, and community responsibility
$ Given: 262 grants totaling $1,042,945; range, $13-$89,000
Application: Initial approach by letter
Deadline: None
Contact: James F. Cordes, President

A.G. Bishop Charitable Trust
c/o NDB Genesee
Merchants Bank and Trust Company
One East First Street
Flint, MI 48502
(313) 766-8307

Description: Areas of support include health agencies and hospitals, social service and youth agencies, education, and cultural programs
$ Given: 49 grants totaling $227,837; range, $750-$33,300
Application: Initial approach by letter
Deadline: None
Contact: C. Ann Barton, Trust Officer

Herrick Foundation
2500 Comerica Building
Detroit, MI 48226
(313) 963-6420

Description: Funding interests include education (scholarship and capital funds), youth and health service agencies, hospitals, welfare agencies, cultural programs, and Protestant church support
$ Given: 190 grants totaling $10,745,750; range, $500-$1,000,000
Application: Initial approach by letter
Deadline: None
Contact: Catherine R. Cobb

FLOW-THROUGH FUNDING

Keebler Company Foundation
One Hollow Tree Lane
Elmhurst, IL 60126
(708) 833-2900

Description: Funding interests include minority programs, health and human services, and education
$ Given: 239 grants totaling $359,987; range, $10-$34,180
Areas of Support: Illinois, Colorado, Indiana, Maine, Michigan, Minnesota, North Carolina, Pennsylvania, Texas
Application: Initial approach by letter
Deadline: None
Contact: A.G. Bland, Treasurer

Milan (Jack and Florence) Foundation
16500 North Park Drive
Apartment 1708
Southfield, MI 48075

Description: Funds Jewish organizations, health services, and child welfare
$ Given: One grant totaling $105,000
Application: N/A
Deadline: N/A
Contact: N/A

Monsanto Fund
800 North Lindbergh Blvd.
St. Louis, MO 63167
(314) 694-4596

Description: Funding interests include health services, hospitals, social services, youth, education (science and mathematics), and community funds
$ Given: Grants totaling $8,285,748; range, $100-$1,112,000
Areas of Support: Alabama, California, Florida, Georgia, Idaho, Illinois, Massachusetts, Maine, Michigan, Missouri, New Jersey, North Carolina, Ohio, South Carolina, Texas, and West Virginia
Application: Proposal
Deadline: None
Contact: John L. Mason, President

• •

MINNESOTA

The Blandin Foundation
100 Pokegama Avenue No.
Grand Rapids, MN 55744
(612) 224-5463

Description: Funding interests include leadership development, economic development, health and human services, educational opportunities, the environment, and arts and humanities
$ Given: 467 grants totaling $293,669; range, $167-$2,417
Areas of Support: Rural Minnesota
Application: Initial approach by letter
Deadline: February 1, May 1, August 1, November 1
Contact: Paul M. Olsen, President

Carolyn Foundation
1800 TCF Tower
Minneapolis, MN 55402
(612) 339-7101

Description: Funding for health and welfare, education, culture, women, the environment, and the disadvantaged
$ Given: 37 grants totaling $989,665; range, $1,300-$100,000
Areas of Support: Minneapolis-St. Paul, Minnesota and New Haven, Connecticut
Application: Initial approach by letter
Deadline: January and February for grants under $10,000; January through July for grants over $10,000
Contact: Carol J. Fetzer, Executive Director

Dain Bosworth/IFG Foundation
100 Dain Tower
Minneapolis, MN 55402
(612) 371-2765

Description: Areas of support include health, education, social service, and community funds
$ Given: 510 grants totaling $350,095; range, $25-$56,000
Application: Initial approach by letter
Deadline: January 31, July 31
Contact: Beth James, Executive Director

FLOW-THROUGH FUNDING

• • • • • • • • • • • • • • • • • •

The Donaldson Foundation
c/o Donaldson Company, Inc.
P.O. Box 1299
Minneapolis, MN 55440
(612) 887-3010

Description: Funding interests include health services, environmental protection, and higher education
$ Given: 98 grants totaling $338,875; range, $300-$38,400
Areas of Support: Illinois, Indiana, Iowa, Kentucky, Minnesota, Missouri, and Wisconsin
Application: Initial approach by letter
Deadline: May 1, August 1
Contact: Raymond Vodovnik, Secretary

Keebler Company Foundation
One Hollow Tree Lane
Elmhurst, IL 60126
(312) 833-2900

Description: Funding interests include minority programs, health and human services, and education
$ Given: 239 grants totaling $359,987; range, $10-$34,180
Areas of Support: Illinois, Colorado, Indiana, Maine, Minnesota, North Carolina, Pennsylvania, Texas
Application: Initial approach by letter
Deadline: None
Contact: A.G. Bland, Treasurer

MISSISSIPPI

Arkla Corporate Giving Program
400 East Capitol Avenue
P.O. Box 751
Little Rock, AK 72203
(501) 377-4610

Description: Funds a wide variety of programs, including health services, mental health, AIDS, child welfare and drug abuse.
$ Given: N/A
Limitations: Giving in major operating areas (Arkansas, California, Kansas, Texas, Oklahoma, and Mississippi)
Application: Initial approach by letter
Deadline: None
Contact: James L. Rutherford III, Senior Vice President (Little Rock, Arkansas area) or Hugh H. McCastlain (Shreveport, Louisiana area)

• • • • • • • • • • • • • • • • • • •

W.E. Walker Foundation
1675 Lakeland Drive
Riverhill Tower
Suite 400
Jackson, MS 39216
(601) 362-9895

Description: Areas of support include health, cultural programs, youth and welfare agencies, and education
$ Given: 56 grants totaling $2,639,275; average range, $1,000-$15,000
Application: Initial approach by letter
Deadline: None
Contact: W.E. Walker, Jr., Trustee

MISSOURI

The H & R Block Foundation
4410 Main Street
Kansas City, MO 64111
(816) 753-6900

Description: Areas of support include health, the elderly, youth, education, arts and culture, and neighborhood development
$ Given: 246 grants totaling $958,751
Application: Initial approach by letter (1-2 pages)
Deadline: 45 days prior to board meetings (board meets in March, June, September, and December
Contact: Terrence R. Ward, President

The Donaldson Foundation
c/o Donaldson Company, Inc.
P.O. Box 1299
Minneapolis, MN 55440
(612) 887-3010

Description: Funding interests include health services, environmental protection, and higher education
$ Given: 98 grants totaling $338,875; range, $300-$38,400
Areas of Support: Illinois, Indiana, Iowa, Kentucky, Minnesota, Missouri, and Wisconsin
Application: Initial approach by letter
Deadline: May 1, August 1
Contact: Raymond Vodovnik, Secretary

The Green (Allen P. and Josephine B.) Foundation
P.O. Box 523
Mexico, MO 65265
(314) 581-5568

Description: Funds health care and educational programs for children and youth, social services, and arts and other cultural programs
$ Given: 47 grants totaling $500,600; range, $1,000-$30,000
Application: Initial approach by letter
Deadline: April 1, October 1
Contact: Walter G. Staley, Secretary-Treasurer

FLOW-THROUGH FUNDING

• • • • • • • • • • • • • • • • • • • •

Group Health Plan Foundation of Greater St. Louis
1056 Caroline Street
St. Louis, MO 63104
(314) 577-8105

Description: Funds health agencies and health services
$ Given: Eight grants totaling $204,975; range, $15,000-$55,000
Application: Initial approach by letter
Deadline: None
Contact: Robert M. Swanson, Secretary

Ewing Marion Kauffman Foundation
922 Walnut Street
Suite 1100
Kansas City, MO 64106
(816) 966-4000

Description: Funds health agencies, childhood education, and family services
$ Given: 20 grants totaling $201,639; range, $50-$75,000
Areas of Support: Kansas and Missouri
Application: Brief concept paper
Deadline: None
Contact: Carl Mitchell, Treasurer

Monsanto Fund
800 North Lindbergh Blvd.
St. Louis, MO 63167
(314) 694-4596

Description: Funding interests include health services, hospitals, social services, youth, education (science and mathematics), and community funds
$ Given: Grants totaling $8,285,748; range, $100-$1,112,000
Areas of Support: Alabama, California, Florida, Georgia, Idaho, Illinois, Massachusetts, Maine, Missouri, New Jersey, North Carolina, Ohio, South Carolina, Texas, and West Virginia
Application: Proposal
Deadline: None
Contact: John L. Mason, President

Olin (Spencer T. and Ann W.) Foundation
Pierre Laclede Building
7701 Forsyth Boulevard
St. Louis, MO 63105
(314) 727-6202

Description: Funding interests include health services, medical education and research, and community service agencies
$ Given: 23 grants totaling $5,454,050; range, $750-$1,500,000
Application: Initial approach by letter
Deadline: None
Contact: Warren M. Shapleigh, President

The Retirement Research Foundation
1300 West Higgins Rd.
Suite 214
Park Ridge, IL 60068
(708) 823-4133

Description: Focus is the improvement of the quality of life of older persons in the United States.
$ Given: Grants totaling $4,131,981; average, $25,000
Areas of Support: Florida, Illinois, Indiana, Iowa, Kentucky, Missouri, and Wisconsin
Application: Initial approach by letter
Deadlines: February 1, May 1, and August 1
Contact: Marilyn Hennessy, Senior Vice President

Victor E. Speas Foundation
c/o Boatmen's First
National Bank of
Kansas City
14 West Tenth Street
Kansas City, MO 64183

Description: Areas of support include agencies serving the health care needs of youth, elderly, and handicapped
$ Given: 38 grants totaling $1,262,212; range, $1,500-$172,000
Application: Initial approach by telephone
Deadline: None
Contact: David P. Ross, Senior Vice President, Boatmen's First National Bank of Kansas City

Speas (John W. and Effie E.) Foundation
c/o Boatmen's First
National Bank of
Kansas City
14 West Tenth Street
Kansas City, MO 64183

Description: Funds hospitals and health services
$ Given: 28 grants totaling $1,189,129; range, $5,000-$152,000
Application: Initial approach by letter (1-3 pages)
Deadline: None
Contact: David P. Ross, Senior Vice President, Boatmen's First National Bank of Kansas City

St. Louis Community Foundation
818 Olive Street
Suite 317
St. Louis, MO 63101
(314) 241-2703

Description: Funding interests include care of the sick, aged, infirm, and handicapped
$ Given: 249 grants totaling $844,231; range, $100-$200,000
Application: Proposal
Deadline: January 15, April 15, July 15, and October 15
Contact: Mary Brucker, Executive Director

• • • • • • • • • • • • • • • • • • •

MONTANA

Meyer Memorial Trust
1515 S.W. Fifth Avenue
Suite 500
Portland, OR 97201
(503) 228-5512

Description: General purpose grants in Oregon for education, health and social welfare, arts and humanities; special program grants for Aging and Independence and Support for Children at Risk in Oregon, Alaska, Idaho, Montana, and Washington; operates a Small Grants Program ($500-$8,000) for small projects in Oregon
$ Given: 209 grants totaling $11,953,746; range, $500-$2,000,000
Application: Application form required
Deadline: April 1, October 1 for Aging and Independence; July 15, October 15 for Small Grants Program; no deadline for general purpose grants
Contact: Charles S. Rooks, Executive Director

MPCo/Entech Foundation, Inc.
c/o The M-P-Co.
40 East Broadway
Butte, Montana 59701
(406) 723-5421

Description: Funding for human services, youth organizations, hospitals, and health associations
$ Given: 34 grants totaling $310,159; range, $50-$76,034
Application: Application form required
Deadline: None
Contact: John Carl, Vice President

NEBRASKA

Thomas D. Buckley Trust
P.O. Box 647
Chappell, NE 69129
(308) 874-2211

Description: Areas of support include health services and hospitals, community development programs, Christian churches, and civic affairs
$ Given: 58 grants totaling $266,736; range, $250-$35,000
Application: Initial approach by letter
Deadline: None
Contact: Dwight E. Smith

• • • • • • • • • • • • • • • • • •

The IBP Foundation, Inc.
P.O. Box 515
Dakota City, NE 68731
(402) 494-2061

Description: Areas of support include community development and health services
$ Given: Grants totaling $219,916
Application: Application form required
Deadline: None
Contact: George S. Spencer, Chair

The Livingston (Milton S. and Corinne N.) Foundation, Inc.
1125 South 103rd St.
Suite 600
Omaha, NE 68124
(402) 558-1112

Description: Funds local Jewish welfare funds, education, culture, and health services
$ Given: 64 grants totaling $361,522; range, $100-$100,000
Application: Initial approach by letter
Deadline: None
Contact: Yale Richards, Executive Director

NEW HAMPSHIRE

Alexandra Eastman Foundation
c/o New Hampshire Charitable Fund
One South Street
P.O. Box 1335
Concord, New Hampshire 03302
(603) 225-6641

Description: Seeks to improve the quality and availability of health care and to promote the health and well-being of residents of the greater Derry, New Hampshire area
$ Given: 13 grants totaling $125,806; range, $2,400-$30,000
Application: Initial approach by letter
Deadline: February 1, May 1, August 1, November 1
Contact: Deborah Cowan, Program Director

Foundation for Seacoast Health
P.O. Box 4606
Portsmouth,
New Hampshire 03801
(603) 433-4001

Description: Supports and promotes health care for infants, adolescents, and the elderly
$ Given: 32 grants totaling $634,808; range, $500-$125,000
Application: Initial approach by letter (not more than 2 pages)
Deadline: March 1 (infant/child health); June 1 (adolescent health); September 1 (elderly health); December 1 (medical financial assistance)
Contact: N/A

FLOW-THROUGH FUNDING

. . . .

Agnes M. Lindsay Trust
45 Market Street
Manchester,
New Hampshire 03101
(603) 669-4140

Description: Funding interests include health services, higher education, services for the handicapped, and welfare institutions
$ Given: 191 grants totaling $863,771 (average range: $1,000-$10,000)
Areas of Support: Maine, Massachusetts, New Hampshire, and Vermont
Application: Proposal
Deadline: None
Contact: Robert L. Chiesa, Trustee

Ellis L. Phillips Foundation
13 Dartmouth College Highway
Lyme, New Hampshire 03768
(603) 795-2790

Description: Areas of support include social services and health care, religion, education, and the arts
$ Given: 38 grants totaling $255,550; range, $600-$50,000
Application: Initial approach by letter (1-3 pages)
Deadline: None
Contact: Patricia A. Cate, Executive Director

Campbell Soup Fund
Campbell Place
Camden, New Jersey 08103
(609) 342-6431

Description: Funding interests include hospitals and other health care facilities, cultural programs, education, social service and youth agencies, and community funds
$ Given: 106 grants totaling $1,869,800; range, $1,300-$200,000
Areas of Support: Camden, New Jersey and Philadelphia, Pennsylvania
Application: Initial approach by letter
Deadline: None
Contact: Frank G. Moore, Vice-Chair

CPC International Corporate Giving Program
International Plaza
P.O. Box 8000
Englewood Cliffs, New Jersey 07632
(201) 894-2336

Description: Areas of support include education, health and welfare, arts and culture, and community programs
$ Given: Grants totaling $646,148; range, $100-$22,000
Application: Initial approach by letter
Deadline: None
Contact: N/A

• • • • • • • • • • • • • • • • • • •

Hagedorn Fund
c/o Manufacturers Hanover
Trust Co.
270 Park Avenue
New York, NY 10017
(212) 270-9107

Description: Funding for education, hospitals and health agencies, the aged, youth agencies, medical research, community funds, and cultural organizations
$ Given: 114 grants totaling $1,110,000; range, $1,000-$85,000
Areas of Support: New York metropolitan area (including New Jersey and Connecticut)
Application: Proposal
Deadline: November 15
Contact: Robert Rosenthal, Vice President, Manufacturers Hanover Trust Company

The Hoyt Foundation
Half Acre Road
Cranbury, New Jersey 08512
(201) 872-2322

Description: Areas of support include health service agencies, hospitals, the handicapped, and education, with emphasis on medical education and research
$ Given: 13 grants totaling $147,000; range, $100-$38,000
Application: Initial approach by letter
Deadline: None
Contact: Charles O. Hoyt, President

Jaqua Foundation
One Garrett Mountain Plaza
West Paterson,
New Jersey 07424
(201) 278-9790

Description: Funds higher education, hospitals, and health services
$ Given: 23 grants totaling $264,900; range, $2,500-$35,000
Application: Initial approach by letter
Deadline: None
Contact: Eli Hoffman, Chair

The Large Foundation
c/o Large, Scammell and
Danziger
117 Main Street
Flemington, New Jersey
08822

Description: Areas of support include health agencies, social service and youth agencies, and historic preservation
$ Given: 39 grants totaling $378,000; range, $500-$125,000
Application: Initial approach by letter
Deadline: Prior to annual meeting (October)
Contact: N/A

FLOW-THROUGH FUNDING

. . . .

Monsanto Fund
800 North Lindbergh Blvd.
St. Louis, MO 63167
(314) 694-4596

Description: Funding interests include health services, hospitals, social services, youth, education (science and mathematics), and community funds
$ Given: Grants totaling $8,285,748; range, $100-$1,112,000
Areas of Support: Alabama, California, Florida, Georgia, Idaho, Illinois, Massachusetts, Maine, Missouri, New Jersey, North Carolina, Ohio, South Carolina, Texas, and West Virginia
Application: Proposal
Deadline: None
Contact: John L. Mason, President

NEW JERSEY

George A. Ohl, Jr., Trust
c/o First Fidelity Bank,
N.A., New Jersey
765 Broad Street
Newark, New Jersey 07102
(201) 430-4237

Description: Funding interests include hospitals and health service agencies, youth projects, and the homeless
$ Given: 38 grants totaling $278,571; range, $500-$93,651
Application: Proposal
Deadline: None
Contact: N/A

Petrie Foundation
70 Enterprise Avenue
Secaucus, New Jersey 07094

Description: Areas of support include cultural programs, religious freedom, hospitals and health services, including physical rehabilitation
$ Given: 67 grants totaling $758,170; range, $500-$108,500
Application: N/A
Deadline: N/A
Contact: N/A

The Rosenhaus (Sarah and Matthew) Peace Foundation
Picatinny Road
Morristown, New Jersey
07960
(201) 267-6583

Description: Promotes world peace and understanding with emphasis on medical research and health services, Jewish organizations, and higher education
$ Given: 39 grants totaling $678,000; range, $200-$100,000
Areas of Support: New Jersey, New York
Application: Applications not accepted; giving to pre-selected organizations
Deadline: N/A
Contact: Irving Rosenhaus, Managing Director

• • • • • • • • • • • • • • •

**Union Camp
Charitable Trust**
c/o Union Camp
Corporation
1600 Valley Road
Wayne, New Jersey 07470
(201) 628-2248

Description: Areas of support include community funds, higher education, hospitals and health services, and cultural programs
$ Given: Grants totaling $1,728,075 (average range: $2,000-$5,000)
Application: Initial approach by letter
Deadline: January through August
Contact: Sydney N. Phin, Director, Human Resources

The Van Houten (Edward W. and Stella C.) Charitable Trust
c/o First Fidelity Bank, N.A., New Jersey
765 Broad Street
Newark, New Jersey 07102
(201) 430-4536

Description: Funds human services, health care and hospitals (preference given to pediatrics), the disabled, and the elderly
$ Given: Grants totaling $1,000,000 (average range: $10,000-$100,000)
Application: Proposal
Deadline: February 15, May 15, August 15, November 15
Contact: James S. Hohn, Assistant Vice President, First Fidelity Bank

NEW MEXICO

FHP Foundation
401 East Ocean Blvd.
Suite 206
Long Beach, CA 90802
(310) 590-8655

Description: Funds direct delivery of health care services, including education programs, programs for the elderly and chronically ill, primary care projects in underserved areas
$ Given: 17 grants totaling $773,064; range, $2,900-$89,000
Areas of Support: Giving in southern California, Utah, New Mexico, Arizona
Application: Initial approach by letter
Deadline: February 15, May 15, August 15, and November 15
Contact: Sandra Lund Gavin, Executive Director

FLOW-THROUGH FUNDING

. . . .

NEW YORK

Albany's Hospital for Incurables
P.O. Box 3628
Executive Park
Albany, NY 12203
(518) 459-7711

Description: Seeks to facilitate development of better health care, including the funding of nursing homes, hospitals, hospices, community health centers, regional health planning groups, and medical colleges
$ Given: 17 grants totaling $249,000; range, $3,000-$30,000
Application: Application form required; initial contact by phone or letter
Deadlines: One month before board meetings (board meets in January, April, June, and November)
Contact: Arnold Cogswell, President

Arkell Hall Foundation, Inc.
66 Montgomery Street
Canajoharie, NY 13317
(518) 673-2281

Description: Operates a residence for needy elderly women who are residents of Montgomery County; funds education, health, and social services
$ Given: 78 grants totaling $618,764; range, $500-$73,633
Application: Form not required
Deadline: September 15
Contact: Joseph A. Santangelo, Administrator

The Barker Welfare Foundation
P.O. Box 2
Glen Head, NY 11545
(516) 759-5592

Description: Funds established organizations in the areas of health services and rehabilitation, child welfare and youth agencies, arts and culture, libraries, family planning, and others
$ Given: 200 grants totaling $1,582,000; range, $1,000-$50,000
Application: Form not required
Deadline: February 1
Contact: Mrs. Walter L. Ross II, President

• • • • • • • • • • • • • • • • • •

The Albert C. Bostwick Foundation
Hillside Avenue and
Bacon Road
P.O. Box A
Westbury, NY 11568
(516) 334-5566

Description: Funds hospitals, health service agencies, handicapped, youth agencies, and medical research
$ Given: 46 grants totaling $114,450; range, $150-$25,000
Application: Initial approach by letter
Deadline: None
Contact: Eleanor P. Bostwich, Trustee

The Brody (Carolyn and Kenneth D.) Foundation
c/o Goldman Sachs and
Company
Tax Department
85 Broad Street
New York, NY 10004

Description: Areas of support include health services, education, cultural programs, and hospitals
$ Given: 99 grants totaling $247,838; range, $15-$25,000
Application: Contributes to pre-selected organizations
Deadline: N/A
Contact: N/A

Central New York Community Foundation, Inc.
600 South Salina St.
Suite 428
Syracuse, NY 13202
(315) 422-9538

Description: Funds existing agencies for health, welfare, educational, recreational, or cultural purposes
$ Given: 324 grants totaling $2,512,360; average range, $200-$15,000
Application: Application form required
Deadlines: 6 weeks before board meetings (board meets March, May, September, and December)
Contact: Margaret G. Ogden, President

Charina Foundation, Inc.
85 Broad Street
New York, NY 10004

Description: Areas of support include arts and culture, health services, community development, welfare funds, recreation, and Jewish organizations
$ Given: 244 grants totaling $504,602; range, $100-$85,000
Application: Applications not accepted; giving to pre-selected organizations
Deadline: N/A
Contact: Richard L. Menschel, President

• • • • • • • • • • • • • • • • • • • •

The Cohen (Saul Z. and Amy Scheuer) Family Foundation, Inc.
c/o 61 Associates
350 Fifth Avenue
Suite 3410
New York, NY 10118

Description: Funds education, Jewish giving, culture, and health services, including mental health
$ Given: 106 grants totaling $2,580,289; range, $50-$1,000,000
Application: Applications not accepted; giving to pre-selected organizations
Deadline: N/A
Contact: N/A

The Commonwealth Fund
One East 75th Street
New York, NY 10021
(212) 535-0400

Description: Areas of support include improving health care service, advancing the well-being of elderly people, developing the capabilities of high school students, and improving the health of minorities
$ Given: Grants totaling $9,622,513; range, $1,000-$595,000
Application: Application form not required; initial approach by letter
Deadline: None
Contact: Adrienne E. Fisher, Grants Manager

The Dreyfus (Max and Victoria) Foundation, Inc.
575 Madison Avenue
New York, NY 10022
(212) 605-0354

Description: Areas of support include health and social services, the aged, handicapped, youth, and cultural programs
$ Given: 225 grants totaling $1,547,416; range, $1,000-$30,000
Application: Initial approach by letter
Deadlines: 10 weeks prior to board meetings (mid-February, June, and October)
Contact: Ms. Lucy Gioia, Administrative Assistant

The Favrot Fund
909 Wirt Road
No. 101
Houston, TX 77024
(713) 956-4009

Description: Focus on community-based programs directed toward health, the needy, and the arts
$ Given: 24 grants totaling $310,000; range, $2,000-$25,000
Areas of Support: Texas, California, New York, and Washington, DC
Application: Initial approach by letter
Deadline: None
Contact: Mrs. Carol Parker

• • • • • • • • • • • • • • • • • •

The Glickenhaus Foundation
100 Dorchester Road
Scarsdale, NY 10583
(212) 953-7800

Description: Funds social welfare, health services, and international peace organizations
$ Given: 222 grants totaling $433,392; range, $16-$100,000
Application: Proposal
Deadline: None
Contact: N/A

Hagedorn Fund
c/o Manufacturers Hanover Trust Co.
270 Park Avenue
New York, NY 10017
(212) 270-9107

Description: Funding for education, hospitals and health agencies, the aged, youth agencies, medical research, community funds, and cultural organizations
$ Given: 114 grants totaling $1,110,000; range, $1,000-$85,000
Areas of Support: New York metropolitan area (including New Jersey and Connecticut)
Application: Proposal
Deadline: November 15
Contact: Robert Rosenthal, Vice President, Manufacturers Hanover Trust Company

The John A. Hartford Foundation, Inc.
55 East 59th Street
New York, NY 10022
(212) 832-7788

Description: Areas of support include aging and health, and health care cost and quality
$ Given: 75 grants totaling $7,335,587; range, $5,000-$600,000
Application: Initial approach by letter or proposal
Deadline: 6 months prior to funding requirements
Contact: Richard S. Sharpe, Program Director

The Howard and Bush Foundation, Inc.
85 Gillett Street
Hartford, CT 06105
(203) 236-8595

Description: Funding emphasis includes health services
$ Given: 77 grants totaling $1,346,985; range, $3,500-$72,052
Areas of Support: Hartford, Connecticut, and Troy, New York
Application: Initial approach by letter
Deadline: February 1, June 1, October 1
Contact: Nancy Roberts

FLOW-THROUGH FUNDING

· · · · · · · · · · · · · · · · · · · ·

The Hoyt Foundation
Half Acre Road
Cranbury, NJ 08512
(201) 872-2322

Description: Areas of support include health service
agencies, hospitals, the handicapped, and education, with
emphasis on medical education and research
$ Given: 13 grants totaling $147,000; range, $100-$38,000
Application: Initial approach by letter
Deadline: None
Contact: Charles O. Hoyt, President

**Sid Jacobson Foundation,
Inc.**
151 Sunnyside Boulevard
Plainview, NY 11803

Description: Funds Jewish concerns, health services,
hospitals and medical research
$ Given: 88 grants totaling $225,900; range, $10-$125,000
Application: Application form not required
Deadline: None
Contact: Sid Jacobson, Trustee

**Key Food Stores
Foundation, Inc.**
8925 Avenue D
Brooklyn, NY 11236
(212) 510-5502

Description: Areas of support include Jewish giving,
health, hospitals, and health clinics
$ Given: 29 grants totaling $110,585; range, $25-$69,000
Application: Application form not required
Deadline: None
Contact: Allen Newman, Trustee

**The Klau (David and
Sadie) Foundation**
c/o Rochlin, Lipsky, Goodkin,
Stoler and Co., P.C.
510 Fifth Avenue
New York, NY 10036
(212) 840-6444

Description: Funding interests include health, AIDS,
education, Jewish welfare funds, child development, and
human services
$ Given: 164 grants totaling $649,249; range, $10-
$200,000
Application: Initial approach by letter
Deadline: None
Contact: Sadie K. Klau, President

• • • • • • • • • • • • • • • • • •

Klock Company Trust
c/o Key Trust Company
253 Wall Street
Kingston, NY 12401
(914) 339-6750

Description: Areas of support include health services, hospitals, social services, youth agencies, education, and cultural programs
$ Given: 28 grants totaling $221,965; range, $1,000-$25,000
Areas of Support: Kingston and Ulster Counties, New York
Application: Initial approach by letter
Deadlines: March, June, September, and December 31
Contact: Earle H. Foster

The Langeloth (Jacob and Valeria) Foundation
One East 42nd Street
New York, NY 10017
(212) 687-3760

Description: Funds non-profit hospitals and health care facilities to defray costs incurred by in-patients who are "people of education" or in the arts who normally would not be justified in accepting charity but who nonetheless would have difficulty meeting their obligations
$ Given: 25 grants totaling $1,451,000; range, $15,000-$100,000
Application: Applications from previous recipients only
Deadline: September 1
Contact: William R. Cross, Jr., President

The Lincoln Fund
292 Madison Avenue
24th Floor
New York, NY 10017
(212) 889-4109

Description: Areas of support include aid to the elderly, education, nursing and medical programs
$ Given: 19 grants totaling $285,000; range, $5,000-$25,000
Application: Initial approach by letter
Deadline: None
Contact: Mrs. James Sargent, President

J.M. McDonald Foundation, Inc.
2057 East River Road
Cortland, NY 13045
(607) 756-9283

Description: Funding interests include the aged, orphans, child welfare, education, health and hospitals
$ Given: 26 grants totaling $405,000; range, $2,500-$30,000
Application: Applications not accepted; giving to pre-selected organizations
Deadline: N/A
Contact: N/A

FLOW-THROUGH FUNDING

• • • • • • • • • • • • • • • • • •

Frederick McDonald Trust
c/o Norstar Trust Company
69 State Street
Albany, NY 12201
(518) 447-4189

Description: Funds hospitals and health service agencies, youth agencies, and a community fund
$ Given: 33 grants totaling $129,500, range, $1,000-$20,000
Application: Application form required
Deadline: October 1
Contact: R.F. Galvin, Senior Trust Officer

Metzger-Price Fund, Inc.
230 Park Avenue
New York, NY 10169
(212) 867-9500

Description: Areas of support include health services, the handicapped, the elderly, child welfare and social service agencies
$ Given: 114 grants totaling $201,000; range, $500-$5,000
Application: Initial approach by letter
Deadlines: One month prior to board meetings (board meets in January, April, July, and October)
Contact: Marie Mallot, Secretary-Treasurer

Morgan Guaranty Trust Company of New York Charitable Trust
60 Wall Street
New York, NY 10260
(212) 648-9673

Description: Areas of support include chronic care management, school health services, and women's centers
$ Given: 349 grants totaling $6,597,039; range, $500-$400,000
Application: Proposal
Deadline: September 15
Contact: Roberta Ruocco, Vice President

New York Foundation
350 Fifth Avenue
No. 2901
New York, NY 10118
(212) 549-8009

Description: Areas of support include programs for the elderly and health services
$ Given: 88 grants totaling $2,318,000; range, $10,000-$50,000
Application: Initial approach by letter
Deadlines: November 1, March 1, and July 1
Contact: Madeline Lee, Executive Director

• •

William S. Paley Foundation, Inc.
51 West 52nd Street
Room 3490
New York, NY 10019
(212) 765-3333

Description: Areas of support include Museum of Television and Radio, education, health services and hospitals, and cultural programs
$ Given: 49 grants totaling $755,150; range, $150-$275,000
Application: Proposal
Deadline: None
Contact: Patrick S. Gallagher, Assistant Secretary

Rochester Area Foundation
335 Main Street East
Suite 402
Rochester, NY 14604
(716) 325-4353

Description: Areas of support include education, health services, cultural programs, and community development
$ Given: 593 grants totaling $1,831,842; range, $100-$80,000
Application: Initial approach by letter
Deadline: Board meets in January, March, May, July, September, and November
Contact: Linda S, Weinstein, President

Helena Rubenstein Foundation, Inc.
405 Lexington Avenue
New York, NY 10174
(212) 896-0806

Description: Emphasis on projects that benefit women and children, including health, community, and social services, and education and the arts
$ Given: Grants totaling $5,035,518; range, $1,500-$300,000
Application: Initial approach by letter
Deadline: None
Contact: Diane Moss, Executive Director

The Spingold (Nate B. and Frances) Foundation, Inc.
c/o Lankenau and Bickford
1740 Broadway
New York, NY 10019

Description: Areas of support include health and human services, with focus on pediatric, geriatric, and gerontological needs
$ Given: Six grants totaling $222,400; range, $12,400-$75,000
Application: Proposal
Deadline: None
Contact: Daniel L. Kurtz, President

FLOW-THROUGH FUNDING

• • • • • • • • • • • • • • • • • • • •

The Seth Sprague Educational and Charitable Foundation
c/o U.S. Trust Company of New York
114 West 147th Street
New York, NY 10036
(212) 852-3683

Description: Areas of support include health and human services, culture and the arts, education, and community development
$ Given: 386 grants totaling $1,560,000; range, $1,000-$25,000
Application: Initial approach by letter
Deadline: April 15, October 15
Contact: Maureen Augusciak, Senior Vice President

Amy Plant Satter Foundation
598 Madison Avenue
9th Floor
New York, NY 10022

Description: Funding interests include health agencies and hospitals, and social services
$ Given: 43 grants totaling $138,000; range, $1,000-$5,000
Application: Initial approach by letter
Deadline: None
Contact: John H. Reilly, Jr., Trustee

Stern (Bernie and Milton) Foundation
335 Madison Avenue
New York, NY 10017
(212) 503-1701

Description: Areas of support include health services, Jewish welfare, and social services
$ Given: 28 grants totaling $239,167; range, $100-$20,000
Application: Application form required
Deadline: N/A
Contact: Bernice Stern, Vice President

Utica Foundation, Inc.
270 Genesee Street
Utica, NY 13502
(315) 735-8212

Description: Funds social and health services, scholarship programs, and cultural programs
$ Given: 44 grants totaling $316,577; range, $700-$72,500
Application: Initial approach by letter
Deadline: N/A
Contact: N/A

Voute (Mary Jane and William J.) Foundation, Inc.
c/o Salomon Brothers, Inc.
One New York Plaza
New York, NY 10004

Description: Funding interests include Catholic church, education, health and social services
$ Given: 82 grants totaling $377,255; range, $10-$30,000
Application: Applications not accepted; giving to pre-selected organizations
Deadline: N/A
Contact: N/A

• •

Lawrence A. Wein Foundation, Inc.
c/o Wein, Malkin and Bettex
60 East 42nd Street
New York, NY 10165

Description: Areas of support include education, Jewish religious and social organizations and welfare funds, health services and hospitals, cultural programs, and social services
$ Given: 275 grants totaling $1,516,020
Application: Initial approach by letter
Deadline: N/A
Contact: Lawrence A. Wein, President

NORTH CAROLINA

Champion McDowell Davis Charitable Foundation
2405 Oleander Drive
Wilmington, NC 28403

Description: Funds health services, care for the elderly, and conservation
$ Given: Six grants totaling $146,870; range, $1,000-$130,000
Application: Initial approach by letter
Deadline: N/A
Contact: Michael C. Brown, President

Close Foundation, Inc.
P.O. Drawer 460
104 East Springs Street
Lancster, SC 29720
(803) 286-2196

Description: Areas of support include health care and community services, education, and recreation
$ Given: 25 grants totaling $391,340; range, $500-$60,000
Areas of Support: Lancaster County, Chester Township of Chester County, Fort Mill Township, South Carolina, and North Carolina
Application: Proposal
Deadline: None
Contact: Charles A. Bundy, President

The Dover Foundation
P.O. Box 208
Shelby, NC 28150
(704) 847-2000

Description: Funding interests include health services, education, church support, museums, and social service agencies
$ Given: 1135 grants totaling $545,000; range, $100-$250,000
Application: Initial approach by letter
Deadline: July
Contact: Hoyt Q. Bailey, President

FLOW-THROUGH FUNDING

• •

The Fullerton Foundation, Inc.
P.O. Box 1146
Gaffney, SC 29342
(803) 489-6678

Description: Funds hospitals, health care, and medical research
$ Given: 34 grants totaling $1,203,000; range, $1,000-$132,900
Areas of Support: South Carolina and North Carolina
Application: Initial approach by letter
Deadline: April 1, August 1
Contact: Walter E. Cavell, Executive Director

James G. Hanes Memorial Fund/Foundation
c/o Wachovia Bank and Trust Company, N.A.
P.O. Box 3099, MC31022
Winston-Salem, NC 27150
(919) 770-5274

Description: Funds health and education projects, conservation, community programs, and cultural programs
$ Given: 39 grants totaling $1,033,830; range, $1,000-$380,000
Application: Proposal
Deadlines: March 15, June 15, September 15, and December 15
Contact: Joyce T. Adger, Vice President, Wachovia Bank and Trust Company

Harris (James J. and Angelia M.) Foundation
P.O. Box 220427
Charlotte, NC 28222
(704) 364-6046

Description: Funding interests include education, health services, Presbyterian churches, and youth and social service agencies
$ Given: 52 grants totaling $755,062; range, $1,000-$50,000
Application: Initial approach by letter (maximum of three pages)
Deadline: None
Contact: Lillian Seaman

Keebler Company Foundation
One Hollow Tree Lane
Elmhurst, IL 60126
(312) 833-2900

Description: Funding interests include minority programs, health and human services, and education
$ Given: 239 grants totaling $359,987; range, $10-$34,180
Areas of Support: Illinois, Colorado, Indiana, Michigan, Minnesota, North Carolina, Pennsylvania, Texas
Application: Initial approach by letter
Deadline: None
Contact: A.G. Bland, Treasurer

• • • • • • • • • • • • • • • • • • • •

Monsanto Fund
800 North Lindbergh Blvd.
St. Louis, Missouri 63167
(314) 694-4596

Description: Funding interests include health services, hospitals, social services, youth, education (science and mathematics), and community funds
$ Given: Grants totaling $8,285,748; range, $100-$1,112,000
Areas of Support: Alabama, California, Florida, Georgia, Idaho, Illinois, Massachusetts, Michigan, Missouri, New Jersey, North Carolina, Ohio, South Carolina, Texas, and West Virginia
Application: Proposal
Deadline: None
Contact: John L. Mason, President

Kate B. Reynolds
Charitable Trust
BB & T Building
Eight West Third Street
Suite M3
Winston-Salem, NC 27101
(919) 723-1456

Description: 75% of income goes to health care for those in need statewide, including services for the aged and those with cancer
$ Given: 97 grants totaling $12,628,574; range, $5,000-$4,500,000
Application: Proposal
Deadline: April 1, October 1
Contact: W. Vance Frye, Executive Secretary

NORTH DAKOTA

Leach (Tom and Frances)
Foundation
P.O. Box 1136
Bismarck, ND 58502
(701) 255-0479

Description: Areas of support include education, hospitals and health services, social service and youth agencies, and cultural programs
$ Given: 41 grants totaling $254,500; range, $500-$50,000
Application: Initial approach by letter
Deadline: October 1
Contact: Clement C. Webster, Executive Director

OHIO

Coshocton Foundation
P.O. Box 15
Coshocton, OH 43812
(614) 622-2532

Description: Funding interests include community improvement, health services, education, and a museum
$ Given: Grants totaling $283,311; range, $1,000-$15,125
Application: Initial approach by letter
Deadline: None
Contact: Orville Fuller, Treasurer

FLOW-THROUGH FUNDING

• • • • • • • • • • • • • • • • • • •

Dana Corporation Foundation
P.O. Box 1000
Toledo, OH 43697
(419) 535-4500

Description: Areas of support include community funds, education, health and social services, youth agencies, and cultural programs
$ Given: 232 grants totaling $1,529,526; range, $100-$161,340
Application: Proposal
Deadline: None
Contact: Pauline Marzollini, Assistant Secretary

The Dayton Foundation
2100 Kettering Tower
Dayton, OH 45423
(513) 222-0410

Description: Areas of support include cultural programs, health and social services, community development, and youth
$ Given: 361 grants totaling $2,232,013; range, $25-$506,501
Application: Initial approach by letter or telephone
Deadlines: March, July, September, and November
Contact: Marilyn Kaplan, Administrative Officer

The Eaton Charitable Fund
Eaton Center
Cleveland, OH 44114
(216) 523-4822

Description: Funding interests include health and human services, medical research, civic and cultural organizations, and independent college funds
$ Given: Grants totaling $3,670,904; average range, $1,000-$10,000
Areas of support include: Areas of company operations
Application: Initial approach by letter or proposal
Deadline: None
Contact: Frederick B. Unger, Director of Community Affairs

The Ford (S.N. and Ada) Fund
c/o Trustcorp Bank, Ohio
42 North Main
Mansfield, OH 44902
(419) 526-3493

Description: Assistance to the aged and the sick; scholarships to the youth of Richland County, Ohio
$ Given: Ten organization grants totaling $36,100; range, $1,000-$7,500; 392 grants to individuals totaling $298,348; range, $16-$11,472
Application: Initial approach by telephone
Deadline: None
Contact: N/A

• • • • • • • • • • • • • • • • • • •

Iowa and Illinois Gas and Electric Company Giving Program
206 East Second Street
Davenport, IA 52802
(319) 326-7038

Description: Areas of support include education, health care, child welfare, civic affairs, community development, and family services
$ Given: 186 grants totaling $ 537,065; range, $10-$106,375
Areas of Support: Davenport, Bettendorf, Cedar Rapids, Iowa City, and Fort Dodge, Iowa; Rock Island and Moline, Illinois; and Ohio
Application: Initial approach by letter
Deadlines: Board meets in January, April, July, and October
Contact: J.C. Decker, Secretary-Treasurer

The Kangesser (Robert E., Harry A., and M. Sylvia) Foundation
1801 East 9th Street
No. 1220
Cleveland, OH 44114
(216) 621-5747

Description: Areas of support include Jewish educational organizations, non-denominational health and medical services, and civic affairs
$ Given: 23 grants totaling $320,000; range, $200-$150,000
Application: Proposal
Deadline: August 31
Contact: David G. Kangesser, President

William H. Kilcawley Fund
c/o The Dollar Savings and Trust Company
P.O. Box 450
Youngstown, OH 44501

Description: Funding interests include programs for the aged and homeless, health and social services, Christian churches, education, and community funds
$ Given: 19 grants totaling $373,700; range, $500-$110,000
Application: Initial approach by letter
Deadline: None
Contact: N/A

The Lincoln Electric Foundation
c/o Society National Bank
22801 St. Clair Avenue
Cleveland, OH 44117
(216) 481-8100

Description: Areas of support include education, a community fund, hospitals and medical services, social service agencies, civic institutions, and cultural programs
$ Given: 40 grants totaling $477,750; range, $250-$115,000
Application: Initial approach by letter
Deadline: September 20
Contact: Ellis F. Smolik, Secretary-Treasurer

FLOW-THROUGH FUNDING

. . . .

David Meade Massie Trust
65 East Second Street
P.O. Box 41
Chillicothe, OH 45601
(614) 772-5070

Description: Funds community development, youth, health, and social service agencies, education, and cultural programs
$ Given: 55 grants totaling $235,671; range, $750-$5,000
Application: Application form required
Deadlines: March 15, June 15, September 15, and December 15
Contact: Marilyn Carnes

Monsanto Fund
800 North Lindbergh Blvd.
St. Louis, Missouri 63167
(314) 694-4596

Description: Funding interests include health services, hospitals, social services, youth, education (science and mathematics), and community funds
$ Given: Grants totaling $8,285,748; range, $100-$1,112,000
Areas of Support: Alabama, California, Florida, Georgia, Idaho, Illinois, Massachusetts, Michigan, Missouri, New Jersey, North Carolina, Ohio, South Carolina, Texas, and West Virginia
Application: Proposal
Deadline: None
Contact: John L. Mason, President

Ohio Bell Foundation
45 Erieview Plaza
Room 870
Cleveland, OH 44114
(216) 822-2423

Description: Funds civic affairs, community development, health, higher, secondary and elementary education, and art and culture
$ Given: 400 grants totaling $2,382,947; range, $100-$500,000
Application: Proposal
Deadline: None
Contact: William W. Boag, Executive Director

The Elisabeth Severance Prentiss Foundation
c/o National City Bank
P.O. Box 5756
Cleveland, OH 44101
(216) 575-2760

Description: Areas of support include hospitals and health institutions in Cuyahoga County, Ohio that are organized and operated exclusively for public charitable purposes
$ Given: 19 grants totaling $2,647,641; range, $5,000-$1,228,740
Application: Proposal
Deadlines: Before May 15 and November 15
Contact: Frank Dinda

P.K. Ranney Foundation
1525 National City Bank Building
Cleveland, OH 44144
(216) 696-4200

Description: Funds a local community foundation, health services, and marine sciences
$ Given: 10 grants totaling $250,000; range, $5,000-$150,000
Application: Proposal
Deadline: None
Contact: Phillip K. Ranney, Secretary

The Richland County Foundation of Mansfield, Ohio
34 1/2 South Park Street
Room 202
Mansfield, OH 44902
(419) 525-3020

Description: Areas of support include health services, hospital additions, education, programs for the indigent aged, youth programs, the handicapped, and the local community fund
$ Given: 43 grants totaling $865,278; range, $35-$187,240
Application: Proposal
Deadline: None
Contact: Betty J. Crawford, Executive Director

The Stouffer Corporation Fund
29800 Bainbridge Road
Solon, OH 44139
(216) 248-3600

Description: Funds higher education, health, community funds, and cultural programs
$ Given: 277 grants totaling $402,550; range, $100-$77,500
Application: Initial approach by letter
Deadline: None
Contact: N/A

FLOW-THROUGH FUNDING

• •

Watson (Walter E. and Caroline H.) Foundation
P.O. Box 450
Youngstown, OH 44501
(216) 744-9000

Description: Funding interests include education, community development, health and human services, child development and youth agencies, and arts and cultural programs
$ Given: 47 grants totaling $238,319; range, $500-$46,000
Application: Application form not required
Deadline: None
Contact: Herbert H. Pridham

OKLAHOMA

Arkla Corporate Giving Program
400 East Capitol Avenue
P.O. Box 751
Little Rock, AK 72203
(501) 377-4610

Description: Funds a wide variety of programs, including health services, mental health, AIDS, child welfare and drug abuse.
$ Given: N/A
Areas of Support: Giving in major operating areas (Arkansas, California, Kansas, Texas, Oklahoma, and Mississippi)
Application: Initial approach by letter
Deadline: None
Contact: James L. Rutherford III, Senior Vice President (Little Rock, Arkansas area) or Hugh H. McCastlain (Shreveport, Louisiana area)

Fort Howard Foundation, Inc.
P.O. Box 11325
Green Bay, WI 54307
(414) 435-8821

Description: Areas of support include education, health care facilities, cultural programs, and social service and youth agencies
$ Given: 6 grants totaling $726,652; range, $13,700-$150,000
Areas of Support: Green Bay, Wisconsin; Muskogee, Oklahoma; and Effingham County, Georgia
Application: The foundation is not presently making any new funding commitments
Contact: Bruce W. Nagel, Executive Director

Gussman (Herbert and Roseline) Foundation
3200 First National Tower
Tulsa, OK 74103

Description: Areas of support include Jewish giving, health services, cultural programs, and educational institutions
$ Given: 56 grants totaling $312,789; range, $25-$220,201
Application: Applications not accepted; giving to pre-selected organizations
Deadline: N/A
Contact: N/A

• •

The Helmerich Foundation
1579 East 21st Street
Tulsa, OK 74114
(918) 742-5531

Description: Large capital funding to Protestant religious organizations, youth and health service agencies, a community development project, and arts and culture
$ Given: Five grants totaling $1,000,000; range, $50,000-$250,000
Application: Initial approach by letter
Deadline: None
Contact: W.H. Helmerich III, Trustee

Public Service Company of Oklahoma Corporate Giving Program
212 East 6th Street
P.O. Box 201
Tulsa, OK 74119
(918) 599-2000

Description: Funding interests include the elderly, child welfare, culture, alcoholism, and education
$ Given: 250 grants totaling $440,000; range, $100-$130,000
Application: Initial approach by letter
Deadline: None
Contact: William R. Stratton, Vice President and C.F.O.

C.W. Titus Foundation
1801 Philtower Building
Tulsa, OK 74103
(918) 582-8095

Description: Funds hospitals and health services, the handicapped, cultural programs, and social service agencies
$ Given: 43 grants totaling $250,269; range, $1,000-$50,000
Application: Application form not required
Deadline: None
Contact: N/A

The William K. Warren Foundation
P.O. Box 470372
Tulsa, OK 74147
(918) 492-8100

Description: Funds local Catholic health care facilities, education, and social services
$ Given: 32 grants totaling $15,389,470; range, $200-$5,700,000
Application: Initial approach by letter
Deadline: None
Contact: W.R. Lissau, President

FLOW-THROUGH FUNDING

. . . .

The Williams Companies Foundation
P.O. Box 2400
Tulsa, OK 74102
(918) 588-2106

Description: Areas of support include health and human services, education, arts and cultural programs, and civic projects
$ Given: Grants totaling $911,368; range, $50-$387,000
Application: Proposal
Deadline: None
Contact: Hannah D. Robson, Manager

OREGON

The Clark Foundation
255 S.W. Harrison Street
GA 2
Portland, OR 97201
(503) 223-5290

Description: Funding interests include medical care, secondary education, youth agencies, cultural programs, and the environment
$ Given: Grants totaling $492,982
Application: Initial approach by letter
Deadline: None
Contact: Jean Ameele

Collins Medical Trust
1618 S.W. First Avenue
Suite 300
Portland, OR 97201
(503) 227-1219

Description: Funds health services and medical research
$ Given: 12 grants totaling $147,385; range, $1,000-$25,000
Application: Initial approach by letter
Deadline: None
Contact: Joseph A. Connolly, Administrator

The William G. Gilmore Foundation
120 Montgomery Street
Suite 1880
San Francisco, CA 94104
(415) 546-1400

Description: Funds community-based organization, including family and social services, health services, and AIDS programs
$ Given: 132 grants totaling $766,345; range, $200-$50,000
Areas of Support: Giving in northern California, Oregon, and Washington.
Application: Initial approach by mail
Deadlines: May 1, November 1
Contact: Faye Wilson, Secretary

. . . .

Louisiana-Pacific Foundation
111 S.W. Fifth Avenue
Portland, OR 97204
(503) 221-0800

Description: Areas of support include health, youth agencies, community funds, education, and the arts
$ Given: 228 grants totaling $780,169; range, $100-$100,000
Application: Initial approach by letter
Deadline: None
Contact: Robert E. Erickson, Trustee

Meyer Memorial Trust
1515 S.W. Fifth Avenue
Suite 500
Portland, OR 97201
(503) 228-5512

Description: General purpose grants in Oregon for education, health and social welfare, arts and humanities; special program grants for Aging and Independence and Support for Children at Risk in Oregon, Alaska, Idaho, Montana, and Washington; operates a Small Grants Program (500-$8,000) for small projects in Oregon
$ Given: 209 grants totaling $11,953,746; range, $500-$2,000,000
Application: Application form required
Deadline: April 1, October 1 for Aging and Independence; July 15, October 15 for Small Grants Program; no deadline for general purpose grants
Contact: Charles S. Rooks, Executive Director

Wheeler Foundation
1211 S.W. Fifth Avenue
Suite 2906
Portland, OR 97204
(503) 228-0261

Description: Areas of support include higher and secondary education, health and medical services and research, cultural programs, and youth agencies
$ Given: 63 grants totaling $240,125; range, $250-$20,000
Application: Initial approach by letter
Deadline: None
Contact: Samuel C. Wheeler, President

PENNSYLVANIA

Bell Telephone Company of Pennsylvania Giving Program
One Parkway
9th Floor "A"
Philadelphia, PA 19102
(215) 466-2257

Description: Funds education, health, welfare, culture and the arts
$ Given: Grants totaling $2,352,947; average range, $1,000-$400,000
Application: Letter, proposal, and IRS 501C3 form demonstrating non-profit status
Deadline: September 30
Contact: Charles D. Fulton, Corporate Contributions Manager

FLOW-THROUGH FUNDING

• •

**Claude Worthington
Benedum Foundation**
1400 Benedum-Trees
Building
Pittsburgh, PA 15222
(412) 288-0360

Description: Funds education, health and human services, community and economic development, and the arts
$ Given: and 107 grants totaling $7,056,551; range, $3,000-$1,000,000
Areas of Support: West Virginia and Greater Pittsburgh, Pennsylvania
Application: Initial approach by letter or telephone
Deadline: None
Contact: Paul R. Jenkins, President

Campbell Soup Fund
Campbell Place
Camden, NJ 08103
(609) 342-6431

Description: Funding interests include hospitals and other health care facilities, cultural programs, education, social service and youth agencies, and community funds
$ Given: 106 grants totaling $1,869,800; range, $1,300-$200,000
Areas of Support: Camden, New Jersey and Philadelphia, Pennsylvania
Application: Initial approach by letter
Deadline: None
Contact: Frank G. Moore, Vice-Chairman

**The Clapp (Anne L. and
George H.) Charitable
and Educational Trust**
c/o Mellon Bank, N.A.
One Mellon Bank Center
Pittsburgh, PA 15230
(412) 234-5598

Description: Areas of support include education, health and social services, hospitals, and a community fund
$ Given: 37 grants totaling $453,500; range, $3,000-$30,000
Application: Initial approach by letter
Deadline: None
Contact: William B. Outy, Vice President, Mellon Bank

Cyclops Foundation
650 Washington Road
Pittsburgh, PA 15228
(412) 343-4000

Description: Areas of support include health services and hospitals, youth and child welfare, the environment, and higher education
$ Given: 56 grants totaling $262,636; range, $500-$50,000
Application: Initial approach by letter
Deadline: None
Contact: Susan R. Knapp, Manager-Cash and Banking

• • • • • • • • • • • • • • • • • • • •

Eden Hall Foundation
Pittsburgh Office and
Research Park
5500 Corporate Drive
Suite 210
Pittsburgh, PA 15237

Description: Funding interests include education, the prevention and alleviation of sickness and disease, and the advancement of good morals
$ Given: 71 grants totaling $3,552,000; range, $2,000-$300,000
Application: Initial approach by letter
Deadline: None
Contact: Arthur H. Andersen, Secretary

Fannie Mae Foundation
3900 Wisconsin Avenue,
N.W.
Washington, DC 20016
(202) 752-6500

Description: Funding interests include housing and community development, and health and social concerns
$ Given: 300 grants totaling $1,151,567; range, $100-$50,000
Areas of Support: Washington, DC; Pasadena, California; Atlanta, Georgia; Chicago, Illinois; and Philadelphia, Pennsylvania
Application: Proposal
Deadline: None
Contact: Harriet M. Ivey, Executive Director

Keebler Company Foundation
One Hollow Tree Lane
Elmhurst, IL 60126
(312) 833-2900

Description: Funding interests include minority programs, health and human services, and education
$ Given: 239 grants totaling $359,987; range, $10-$34,180
Areas of Support: Illinois, Colorado, Indiana, Michigan, Minnesota, North Carolina, Pennsylvania, Texas
Application: Initial approach by letter
Deadline: None
Contact: A.G. Bland, Treasurer

The Lancaster County Fund
Horst Group Building
29 East King Street
Room 14
Lancaster, PA 17602
(717) 397-1629

Description: Funding interests include health services, youth agencies, education, and cultural programs
$ Given: 52 grants totaling $378,012; average range, $3,000-$10,000
Application: Application form required
Deadline: October 15
Contact: Nancy L. Neff, Executive Secretary

FLOW-THROUGH FUNDING

. . . .

**John R. McCune
Charitable Trust**
P.O. Box 1749
Pittsburgh, PA 15230
(412) 644-7664

Description: Funds education, health services, Presbyterian institutions, and social services
$ Given: 63 grants totaling $1,993,900; range, $5,000-$142,500
Application: Proposal
Deadline: May 1
Contact: James M. Edwards, Member, Dispensing Committee

McCune Foundation
1104 Commonwealth
Building
316 Fourth Avenue
Pittsburgh, PA 15222
(412) 644-8779

Description: Areas of support include education, health, social services, and community health centers
$ Given: 37 grants totaling $13,364,994; range, $40,000-$1,500,000
Application: Initial approach by letter
Deadlines: November 1, March 15
Contact: Earland I. Carlson, Executive Director

**R.K. Mellon Family
Foundation**
P.O. Box 1138
Pittsburgh, PA 15230
(412) 392-2800

Description: Funds education, health care, social and human services, and conservation
$ Given: 70 grants totaling $1,103,950; range, $1,000-$100,000
Application: Proposal
Deadlines: April 1, October 1
Contact: Robert B. Burr, Jr., Director

**Mine Safety Appliances
Company Charitable Trust**
c/o Mine Safety Appliances
Company
P.O. Box 426
Pittsburgh, PA 15230

Description: Areas of support include health care, community funds, and education
$ Given: 132 grants totaling $607,818; range, $100-$125,000
Application: Initial approach by letter
Deadline: None
Contact: James E. Herald, Secretary

• • • • • • • • • • • • • • • • • •

**Pittsburgh National Bank
Foundation**
Pittsburgh National Building
14th Floor
Fifth Avenue and Wood St.
Pittsburgh, PA 15222
(412) 762-4222

Description: Funds health services and hospitals,
community funds, social services, education, and youth
agencies
$ Given: 277 grants totaling $1,541,055; range, $25-
$363,500
Application: Initial approach by letter
Deadline: None
Contact: D. Paul Beard, Secretary

Stockpole-Hall Foundation
44 South St. Marys Street
St. Marys, PA 15857
(814) 834-1845

Description: Areas of support include education, youth
and child welfare, health services, and community
development
$ Given: 54 grants totaling $659,768; range, $800-$53,000
Application: Initial approach by letter
Deadline: None
Contact: William C. Conrad, Executive Secretary

**Wilson (Hugh and Mary)
Foundation, Inc.**
c/o Wood and Seitl
240 North Washington Blvd.
Suite 460
Sarasota, FL 34236
(813) 954-2155

Description: Areas of support include cancer research
and health services, the performing arts, and social
service issues
$ Given: 26 grants totaling $238,291; range, $1,000-$50,000
Areas of Support: Manatee-Sarasota, Florida; Lewisburg-
Danville, Pennsylvania
Application: Initial approach by letter
Deadline: None
Contact: John R. Wood, President

RHODE ISLAND

**The Rhode Island
Foundation/The Rhode
Island Community
Foundation**
957 North Main Street
Providence, RI 02904
(401) 274-4564

Description: Funding interests include education, health
care, the aged, youth, and social services
$ Given: Grants totaling $3,381,921
Application: Initial approach by letter or telephone
Deadline: None
Contact: Douglas M. Jansson, Executive Director

FLOW-THROUGH FUNDING

• •

SOUTH CAROLINA

Close Foundation, Inc.
P.O. Drawer 460
104 East Springs Street
Lancster, SC 29720
(803) 286-2196

Description: Areas of support include health care (including cancer) and community services, education, and recreation
$ Given: 25 grants totaling $391,340; range, $500-$60,000
Areas of Support: Lancaster County, Chester Township of Chester County, Fort Mill Township, South Carolina, and North Carolina
Application: Proposal
Deadline: None
Contact: Charles A. Bundy, President

The Fullerton Foundation, Inc.
P.O. Box 1146
Gaffney, SC 29342
(803) 489-6678

Description: Funds hospitals, health care, and medical research
$ Given: 34 grants totaling $1,203,000; range, $1,000-$132,900
Areas of Support: South Carolina and North Carolina
Application: Initial approach by letter
Deadline: April 1, August 1
Contact: Walter E. Cavell, Executive Director

Monsanto Fund
800 North Lindbergh Boulevard
St. Louis, Missouri 63167
(314) 694-4596

Description: Funding interests include health services, hospitals, social services, youth, education (science and mathematics), and community funds
$ Given: Grants totaling $8,285,748; range, $100-$1,112,000
Areas of Support: Alabama, California, Florida, Georgia, Idaho, Illinois, Massachusetts, Michigan, Missouri, New Jersey, North Carolina, Ohio, South Carolina, Texas, and West Virginia
Application: Proposal
Deadline: None
Contact: John L. Mason, President

• • • • • • • • • • • • • • • • • • • •

Post and Courier Foundation
134 Columbus Street
Charleston, SC 29403
(803) 577-7111

Description: Areas of support include community development, health services, and cultural programs
$ Given: 98 grants totaling $472,364; range, $50-$76,707
Application: Proposal
Deadline: None
Contact: J.F. Smoak, Foundation Manager

The Self Foundation
P.O. Drawer 1017
Greenwood, SC 29648
(803) 229-2571

Description: Focus on health care and higher education, with some support for cultural programs, youth, and the elderly
$ Given: 28 grants totaling $1,032,817; range, $500-$125,000
Application: Proposal
Deadline: March 1, June 1, September 1, and December 1
Contact: Frank J. Wideman, Jr., Executive Vice President

TENNESSEE

Christy-Houston Foundation
122 North Spring Street
Murfreesboro, TN 37130
(615) 898-1140

Description: Funds hospitals and health-related projects
$ Given: Five grants totaling $158,245; range, $16,000-$49,860
Application: Application form not required
Deadline: January 31
Contact: James R. Arnhart, Executive Director

Hargis (Estes H. and Florence Parker) Charitable Foundation
317 20th Street North
P.O. Box 370404
Birmingham, AL 35237
(205) 251-2881

Description: Funding for health and youth services
$ Given: 7 grants totaling $395,374; range, $300-$376,075
Areas of Support: Alabama, Tennessee
Application: Initial approach by letter
Deadline: May 1
Contact: Gerald D. Colvin, Jr., Chair

FLOW-THROUGH FUNDING

• • • • • • • • • • • • • • • • • • • •

The William B. Stokely, Jr. Foundation
620 Campbell Station Road
Station West
Suite Y
Knoxville, Tennessee 37922
(615) 966-4878

Description: Areas of support include education, health services, and cultural programs
$ Given: 96 grants totaling $415,000; range, $50-$50,000
Application: Initial approach by letter or proposal
Deadline: N/A
Contact: William B. Stokely III, President

Washington Foundation
3815 Cleghorn Avenue
P.O. Box 159057
Nashville, TN 37215
(615) 244-0600

Description: Church of Christ-related organizations in the areas of health and welfare
$ Given: 132 grants totaling $682,450; range, $200-$65,000
Application: Initial approach by letter
Deadline: December 1
Contact: Paul A. Hargis, President

TEXAS

Abell-Hanger Foundation
303 West Wall
Room 615
Midland, TX 79701
(915) 684-6655

Description: Areas of support include education, health services, cultural programs, youth activities, and social welfare agencies
$ Given: 110 grants totaling $3,827,099; range, $1,000-$600,000
Application: Application form required
Deadlines: September 30, January 31, and May 31
Contact: David L. Smith, Manager

Arkla Corporate Giving Program
400 East Capitol Avenue
P.O. Box 751
Little Rock, AR 72203
(501) 377-4610

Description: Funds a wide variety of programs, including health services, mental health, AIDS, child welfare and drug abuse.
$ Given: N/A
Limitations: Giving in major operating areas (Arkansas, California, Kansas, Texas, Oklahoma, and Mississippi)
Application: Initial approach by letter
Deadline: None
Contact: James L. Rutherford III, Senior Vice President (Little Rock, Arkansas area) or Hugh H. McCastlain (Shreveport, Louisiana area)

The Cain (Effie and Wofford) Foundation
6116 North Central Expressway
Suite 909-LB65
Dallas, TX 75206
(214) 361-4201

Description: Funding interests include religious organizations, medical services and research, including cancer counseling, and education
$ Given: 56 grants totaling $1,615,230; range, $500-$500,000
Application: Application form required
Deadline: August 31
Contact: Harvey L. Walker, Executive Director

Amon G. Carter Foundation
1212 North Carolina
NB Center
P.O. Box 1036
Fort Worth, TX 76101
(817) 332-2783

Description: Funds arts, health care, education, programs for the aged, and youth agencies
$ Given: 115 grants totaling $8,532,113; range, $500-$3,918,902
Application: Initial approach by letter
Deadline: None
Contact: Bob J. Crowe, Executive Director

Dodge Jones Foundation
P.O. Box 176
Abilene, TX 79604
(915) 673-6429

Description: Areas of support include education, the arts, health, community funds, and youth services
$ Given: 94 grants totaling $2,465,387; range, $100-$500,000
Application: Initial approach by letter
Deadline: None
Contact: Lawrence E. Gill, Vice President, Grants Administration

The Fasken Foundation
500 West Texas Avenue
Suite 1160
Midland, TX 79701
(915) 683-5401

Description: Funding interests include health and social services (including hospices and programs for alcoholism),and education
$ Given: 72 grants totaling $1,028,066; range, $1,000-$105,000
Application: Initial approach by letter
Deadline: December or July
Contact: B.L. Jones, Executive Director

FLOW-THROUGH FUNDING

. . . .

The Favrot Fund
909 Wirt Road
No. 101
Houston, TX 77024
(713) 956-4009

Description: Focus on community-based programs directed toward health, the needy, and the arts
$ Given: 24 grants totaling $310,000; range, $2,000-$25,000
Areas of Support: Texas, California, New York, and Washington, DC
Application: Initial approach by letter
Deadline: None
Contact: Mrs. Carol Parker

The Fondren Foundation
Texas Commerce Tower
Trust Dept., 7th Floor
P.O. Box 2558
Houston, TX 77252
(713) 236-4403

Description: Areas of support include education, health, social service and youth agencies, and cultural organizations
$ Given: 63 grants totaling $3,201,750; range, $1,000-$500,000
Application: Initial approach by letter
Deadline: None
Contact: Melanie A. Boone, Assistant Secretary

The Frees Foundation
5373 West Alabama
Suite 404
Houston, TX 77056
(713) 623-0515

Description: Emphasis on community organizations in Texas and the Republic of Mexico; support includes hospitals and health services
$ Given: 13 grants totaling $153,571; range, $300-$100,000
Application: Proposal
Deadline: None
Contact: Nancy Frees Rosser, Director

The Green Foundation
3300 First City Center
Dallas, TX 75201
(214) 969-1700

Description: Areas of support include hospitals and medical service, cultural programs, education, and a community fund
$ Given: 26 grants totaling $482,150; range, $250-$150,000
Application: Application form not required
Deadline: None
Contact: William E. Collins, Trustee

The Hamman (George and Mary Josephine) Foundation
910 Travis Street
No. 1438
Houston, TX 77002
(713) 658-8345

Description: Funding interests include medical treatment, hospital contruction, education, and social service
$ Given: Grants totaling $637,400; range, $500-$65,000
Application: Initial approach by letter
Deadline: None
Contact: Stephen I. Gelsey, Administrator

Hawn Foundation
1540 Republic Bank Building
Dallas, TX 75201
(214) 220-2828

Description: Areas of support include health service, medical research, education, and cultural programs
$ Given: 41 grants totaling $782,000; range, $500-$250,000
Application: Initial approach by letter
Deadline: None
Contact: E.S. Blythe, Secretary-Treasurer

Hoblitzelle Foundation
1410 Tower 1
NCNB Center
Dallas, TX 75201
(214) 979-0321

Description: Funds education, hospitals and health services, cultural programs, and community development
$ Given: 59 grants totaling $3,289,518; range, $200-$300,000
Application: Initial approach by letter
Deadline: April 15, August 15, December 15
Contact: Paul W. Harris, Executive Vice President

Keebler Company Foundation
One Hollow Tree Lane
Elmhurst, IL 60126
(312) 833-2900

Description: Funding interests include minority programs, health and human services, and education
$ Given: 239 grants totaling $359,987; range, $10-$34,180
Areas of Support: Illinois, Colorado, Indiana, Michigan, Minnesota, North Carolina, Pennsylvania, Texas
Application: Initial approach by letter
Deadline: None
Contact: A.G. Bland, Treasurer

FLOW-THROUGH FUNDING

. . . .

Oliver Dewey Mayor Foundation
c/o AmeriTrust Texas, N.A.
P.O. Box 1088
Sherman, TX 75091
(214) 868-0819

Description: Areas of support include community development, health and social services, education, and youth
$ Given: Grants totaling $278,581
Application: Proposal
Deadline: None
Contact: Philip McKenzie, Trust Officer, AmeriTrust Texas, N.A.

Monsanto Fund
800 North Lindbergh
Boulevard
St. Louis, Missouri 63167
(314) 694-4596

Description: Funding interests include health services, hospitals, social services, youth, education (science and mathematics), and community funds
$ Given: Grants totaling $8,285,748; range, $100-$1,112,000
Areas of Support: Alabama, California, Florida, Georgia, Idaho, Illinois, Massachusetts, Michigan, Missouri, New Jersey, North Carolina, Ohio, South Carolina, Texas, and West Virginia
Application: Proposal
Deadline: None
Contact: John L. Mason, President

The Moody Foundation
704 Moody National Bank
Building
Galveston, TX 77550
(409) 763-5333

Description: Funding interests include health services (including pediatric cardiology), education, and community and social services
$ Given: 79 grants totaling $15,460,064; average range, $10,000-$150,000
Application: Initial approach by letter or telephone
Deadline: Six weeks prior to quarterly board meetings
Contact: Peter M. Moore, Grants Officer

Dora Roberts Foundation
c/o Texas American Bridge
Bank/Fort Worth
P.O. Box 2050
Fort Worth, TX 76113
(817) 884-4442

Description: Areas of support include education, health services and hospitals, Protestant church support, and youth agencies
$ Given: Grants totaling $874,294; range, $780-$230,000
Application: Proposal
Deadline: September 30
Contact: Rick Piersall, Vice President and Trust Officer

• • • • • • • • • • • • • • • •

Semmes Foundation
800 Navarro
Suite 210
San Antonio, TX 78205
(512) 225-0887

Description: Funds education, health services, the arts and museums
$ Given: 29 grants totaling $349,948; range, $100-$151,150
Application: Initial approach by letter
Deadline: None
Contact: Thomas R. Semmes, President

T.L.L. Temple Foundation
109 Temple Boulecard
Lufkin, TX 75901
(409) 639-5197

Description: Areas of support include education, health services, and community and social services
$ Given: 178 grants totaling $10,009,877; range, $1,000-$1,250,000
Application: Initial approach by letter
Deadline: None
Contact: Ward R. Burke, Executive Secretary

Turner Charitable Foundation
811 Rusk Street
Suite 205
Houston, TX 77002
(713) 237-1117

Description: Funding interests include education, hospitals and health services, Catholic, Protestant, and Jewish church support, social service and youth agencies, and arts and cultural programs
$ Given: 57 grants totaling $426,100; range, $100-$75,000
Application: Initial approach by letter
Deadline: March 15
Contact: Eyvonne Moser, Assistant Secretary

The Vale-Asche Foundation
910 River Oaks Bank Building
2001 Kirby Drive
Suite 910
Houston, TX 77019
(713) 520-7334

Description: Funds health care, medical research, aid to the aged and handicapped, and child welfare
$ Given: 19 grants totaling $225,129; range, $1,000-$30,000
Application: Initial approach by letter
Deadline: None
Contact: Mrs. Vale Asche Akerman, President

FLOW-THROUGH FUNDING

· · · · · · · · · · · · · · · · · · · ·

**Crystelle Waggoner
Charitable Trust**
c/o Texas National Bank
P.O. Box 1317
Fort Worth, TX 76101
(817) 390-6114

Description: Areas of support include health services and associations, arts and cultural programs, and social services
$ Given: 55 grants totaling $286,224; range, $50-$37,000
Application: Initial approach by letter
Deadline: March 31, June 30, September 30, December 31
Contact: Darlene Mann, Vice President, North CarolinaNB Texas National Bank

**Lola Wright Foundation,
Inc.**
P.O. Box 1138
Georgetown, TX 78627
(512) 255-3067

Description: Focus on social service, health and hospitals, the aged, cultural programs, and community funds
$ Given: Grants totaling $564,884; average range, $1,500-$25,000
Application: Initial approach by letter
Deadline: None
Contact: N/A

UTAH

**The Dumke (Dr. Ezekial
R. and Edna Wattis)
Foundation**
600 Crandall Building
10 West First South
Salt Lake City, UT 84101
(801) 363-7863

Description: Funds education, medical and hospital services, youth agencies, and cultural programs
$ Given: 27 grants totaling $262,113; range, $1,000-$40,000
Areas of Support: Utah and Illinois
Application: Application form required
Deadline: February 1, July 1
Contact: Max B. Lewis, Secretary

**Willard L. Eccles
Charitable Foundation**
P.O. Box 45385
Salt Lake City, UT 84145
(801) 532-1500

Description: Areas of support include
$ Given: 15 grants totaling $1,000,383; range, $2,000-$235,000
Application: Initial approach by letter
Deadline: Month preceeding board meetings (board meets in March, June, and October)
Contact: Clark P. Giles, Secretary

· · · · · · · · · · · · · · · · · ·

FHP Foundation
401 East Ocean Boulevard
Suite 206
Long Beach, CA 90802
(310) 590-8655

Description: Funds direct delivery of health care services, including education programs, programs for the elderly and chronically ill, and primary care projects in underserved areas.
$ Given: 17 grants totaling $773,064; range, $2,900-$89,000
Areas of Support: Giving in southern California, Utah, New Mexico, Arizona
Application: Initial approach by letter
Deadline: February 15, May 15, August 15, and November 15
Contact: Sandra Lund Gavin, Executive Director

Questar Corporate Giving Program
180 East First South Street
P.O. Box 11150
Salt Lake City, UT 84147
(801) 534-5435

Description: Funding interests include the aged, medical and health services, education, the disadvantaged, and arts and culture
$ Given: Grants totaling $330,000
Application: Initial approach by letter
Deadline: None
Contact: Janice Bates, Director of Community Affairs

VERMONT

Agnes M. Lindsay Trust
45 Market Street
Manchester, NH 03101
(603) 669-4140

Description: Funding interests include health services, higher education, services for the handicapped, and welfare institutions
$ Given: 191 grants totaling $863,771; average range, $1,000-$10,000
Areas of Support: Maine, Massachusetts, New Hampshire, and Vermont
Application: Proposal
Deadline: None
Contact: Robert L. Chiesa, Trustee

National Life Insurance Corporate Contributions Program
National Life Drive
Montpelier, VT 05604
(802) 229-3333

Description: Areas of support include health, education, arts and culture, and civic and community affairs
$ Given: 150 grants totaling $161,000; range, $50-$15,000
Application: Initial approach by letter
Deadline: None
Contact: Jane W. Robb, Communications Associate

. . . .

VIRGINIA

Cartledge Charitable Foundation, Inc.
P.O. Box 12528
Roanoke, VA 24026
(703) 343-1701

Description: Funding interests include education, health services, and youth organizations
$ Given: 117 grants totaling $233,734; range, $25-$30,000
Application: Initial approach by letter
Deadline: None
Contact: N/A

Massey Foundation
P.O. Box 26765
Richmond, VA 23261
(804) 788-1800

Description: Areas of support include education, health services and hospitals, social services, and cultural programs
$ Given: 76 grants totaling $1,367,250; range, $1,000-$210,000
Application: Initial approach by letter
Deadline: None
Contact: William E. Massey, Jr., President

Universal Leaf Foundation
P.O. Box 25099
Richmond, VA 23260
(804) 359-9311

Description: Funding interests include education, health, medical research, youth agencies, and the arts
$ Given: 175 grants totaling $354,176; range, $75-$31,000
Application: Initial approach by letter
Deadline: None
Contact: Nancy G. Powell, Manager of Corporate Relations

Wheat Foundation
707 East Main Street
Richmond, VA 23219
(804) 649-2311

Description: Funds higher and secondary education, cultural programs, health services, and hospitals
$ Given: 160 grants totaling $340,000; range, $500-$100,000
Areas of Support: Virginia, Washington, DC, Delaware, Georgia, Maryland, North Carolina, Pennsylvania, and West Virginia
Application: Initial approach by letter or telephone
Deadline: None
Contact: William V. Daniel, Treasurer and Trustee

WASHINGTON

The William G. Gilmore Foundation
120 Montgomery Street
Suite 1880
San Francisco, CA 94104
(415) 546-1400

Description: Funds community-based organization, including family and social services, health services, and AIDS programs
$ Given: 132 grants totaling $766,345; range, $200-$50,000
Areas of Support: Giving in northern California, Oregon, and Washington
Application:
Deadlines: May 1, November 1
Contact: Faye Wilson, Secretary

Glaser Foundation, Inc.
P.O. Box N
Edmonds, WA 98020

Description: Areas of support include direct-line service health agencies, drug abuse programs, the aged, the indigent, youth, and the handicapped
$ Given: 62 grants totaling $236,772; range, $50-$10,245
Application: Application form required; Initial approach by letter
Deadline: None
Contact: R.W. Carlstrom, Executive Director

Joshua Green Foundation, Inc.
1414 Fourth Avenue
P.O. Box 720
Seattle, WA 98111
(206) 344-2285

Description: Funding interests include education, health services and agencies, community funds, and church support
$ Given: 60 grants totaling $269,423; range, $200-$80,000
Application: Proposal
Deadline: None
Contact: N/A

George Frederick Jewett Foundation
One Maritime Plaza
Suite 990
San Francisco, CA 94111
(415) 421-1351

Description: Interests include health care and medical research and services
$ Given: 134 grants totaling $953,597; range, $500-$25,000
Areas of Support: San Francisco, California; eastern Washington; northern Idaho
Application: Initial approach by letter
Deadlines: February 15, May 15, August 15, and November 1
Contact: Theresa A. Mullen, Program Director

FLOW-THROUGH FUNDING

• • • • • • • • • • • • • • • • • • • •

Lockwood (Byron W. and Alice L.) Foundation
8121 S.E. 44th Street
Mercer Island, WA 98040
(206) 232-1881

Description: Funds health, culture, education, and youth and social service organizations
$ Given: 38 grants totaling $418,800; range, $500-$100,000
Application: Initial approach by letter
Deadline: N/A
Contact: Sally Easterbrook

Meyer Memorial Trust
1515 S.W. Fifth Avenue
Suite 500
Portland, OR 97201
(503) 228-5512

Description: General purpose grants in Oregon for education, health and social welfare, arts and humanities; special program grants for Aging and Independence and Support for Children at Risk in Oregon, Alaska, Idaho, Montana, and Washington; operates a Small Grants Program (500-$8,000) for small projects in Oregon
$ Given: 209 grants totaling $11,953,746; range, $500-$2,000,000
Application: Application form required
Deadline: April 1, October 1 for Aging and Independence; July 15, October 15 for Small Grants Program; no deadline for general purpose grants
Contact: Charles S. Rooks, Executive Director

Puget Sound Power and Light Corporate Giving Program
P.O. Box 97034
Bellevue, WA 98009
(206) 462-3799

Description: Areas of support include education, health services, hospitals, arts and humanities, and environmental programs
$ Given: 79 grants totaling $597,101; range, $50-$25,000
Application: Initial approach by short letter
Deadline: Late summer and early fall
Contact: Neil L. McReynolds, Senior Vice President, Corporate Relations

Spokane Inland Northwest Community Foundation
400 Paulsen Center
West 421 Riverside Avenue
Spokane, WA 99201
(509) 624-2606

Description: Funding interests include the elderly, music and the arts, social and health services, and education
$ Given: 440 grants totaling $738,429; average grant, $1,500
Areas of Support: The inland northwest (Washington and Idaho)
Application: Initial approach by letter
Deadlines: October 1 (Spokane, Washington); November 1 (Pullman and Dayton, Washington); May 1 (northern Idaho); and October 15 (ISC fund)
Contact: Jeanne L. Ager, Executive Director

• • • • • • • • • • • • • • • • • • • •

Washington Mutual
Savings Bank Foundation
c/o Washington Mutual
Tower
P.O. Box 834
1201 Third Avenue
Seattle, WA 98111
(206) 461-4663

Description: Areas of support include health and welfare, education, cultural enhancement, and civic betterment
$ Given: 176 grants totaling $593,113; range, $500-$40,000
Application: Application form required
Deadline: March 31, June 30, September 31, December 31
Contact: Greg Tuke, Program Administrator

WEST VIRGINIA

Clay Foundation
1426 Kanawha Blvd. East
Charleston, WV 25301
(304) 344-8656

Description: Funds aging, health care, vocational education, and disadvantaged youth
$ Given: 17 grants totaling $905,965; range, $2,000-$300,000
Application: Proposal
Deadline: Write for information
Contact: Betsy B. VonBlond, Executive Director

WISCONSIN

Badger Meter Foundation
4545 West Brown Deer Rd.
Milwaukee, WI 53223
(414) 355-0400

Description: Areas of support include health care, education, community funds, the disabled, and the arts
$ Given: 119 grants totaling $286,200; range, $25-$20,000
Application: Initial approach by letter
Deadline: August 31
Contact: Mary George, Secretary

Chapman Foundation
777 East Wisconsin Avenue
Suite 3090
Milwaukee, WI 53202
(414) 276-6955

Description: Funds education, health services, conservation, and culture
$ Given: 48 grants totaling $246,280; range, $100-$100,000
Application: Applications not accepted; giving to pre-selected organizations
Deadline: N/A
Contact: George M. Chester, President

FLOW-THROUGH FUNDING

• • • • • • • • • • • • • • • • • • • •

John Deere Foundation
John Deere Road
Moline, IL 61265
(309) 765-4137

Description: Areas of support include health services, community funds, youth agencies, and education
$ Given: Grants totaling $3,707,974; range, $300-$539,000
Areas of Support: Iowa, Illinois, Wisconsin
Application: Initial approach by letter
Deadline: None
Contact: Donald R. Morgenthaler, President

The Donaldson Foundation
c/o Donaldson Company, Inc.
P.O. Box 1299
Minneapolis, MN 55440
(612) 887-3010

Description: Funding interests include health services, environmental protection, and higher education
$ Given: 98 grants totaling $338,875; range, $300-$38,400
Areas of Support: Illinois, Indiana, Iowa, Kentucky, Minnesota, Missouri, and Wisconsin
Application: Initial approach by letter
Deadline: May 1, August 1
Contact: Raymond Vodovnik, Secretary

Fort Howard Foundation, Inc.
P.O. Box 11325
Green Bay, WI 54307
(414) 435-8821

Description: Areas of support include education, health care facilities, cultural programs, and social service and youth agencies
$ Given: Six grants totaling $726,652; range, $13,700-$150,000
Areas of Support: Green Bay, Wisconsin; Muskogee, Oklahoma; and Effingham County, Georgia
Application: The foundation is not presently making any new funding commitments
Contact: Bruce W. Nagel, Executive Director

Madison Community Foundation
615 East Washington Ave.
Madison, WI 53703
(608) 255-0503

Description: Funding interests include health and human services, youth, art and culture, education, and econominc development
$ Given: 48 grants totaling $356,826
Application: Initial approach by letter
Deadlines: February 1 for letter of intent; March 15 for proposal
Contact: Jane Taylor Coleman, Executive Director

Faye McBeath Foundation
1020 North Broadway
Milwaukee, WI 53202
(414) 272-2626

Description: Areas of support include homes and care for the elderly, medical, nursing, and hospital care for the sick, and child welfare
$ Given: 53 grants totaling $1,414,337; range, $15,000-$75,000
Application: Initial approach by letter
Deadlines: One month prior to board meetings (board meets bimonthly)
Contact: Sarah M. Dean, Executive Director

Milwaukee Foundation
1020 North Broadway
Milwaukee, WI 53202
(414) 272-5805

Description: Areas of support include health care and hospitals, educational institutions, social services, and arts and cultural programs
$ Given: 429 rants totaling $4,004,551; range, $100-$175,000
Application: Initial approach by letter, proposal, or telephone
Deadlines: January 2, March 1, June 18, September 17, and December 17
Contact: David M.G. Huntington, Executive Director

The Retirement Research Foundation
1300 West Higgins Road
Suite 214
Park Ridge, IL 60068
(708) 823-4133

Description: Focus is the improvement of the quality of life of older persons in the United States.
$ Given: Grants totaling $4,131,981; **average,** $25,000
Areas of Support: Florida, Illinois, Indiana, Iowa, Kentucky, Missouri, and Wisconsin
Application: Initial approach by letter
Deadlines: February 1, May 1, and August 1
Contact: Marilyn Hennessy, Senior Vice President

Time Insurance Foundation
515 West Wells Street
Milwaukee, WI 53203

Description: Funds community service, with emphasis on health care services, education, and the arts
$ Given: 156 grants totaling $294,484; range, $50-$100,000
Application: Initial approach by letter requesting guidelines
Deadline: None
Contact: John E. Krick, President

State and Regional Government Grants

. . . .

This chapter lists state and regional government agencies that can be of assistance in your search for funding. For the most part, these agencies represent a local level of access to federal funding programs and organizations. For example, the Department of Health and Human Services (DHHS) has several regional offices; individuals or groups applying for funds from a DHHS national program (such as "Community Health Centers") must make their applications through their regional offices. Because each government agency administers several different funding programs, and because monies available vary from year to year, the state-by-state information provided here is, for the most part, listed in a generic form. For details about the federal funding programs administered through these regional offices, please refer to the next chapter, "Federal Grants."

Also included in this chapter are Native and Indian Health Service grants, which provide funding for American Indians and Native Alaskans. These grants are administered through local offices serving their immediate areas. Money is awarded directly to federally-recognized tribes or tribal organizations which, in turn, use the money to provide health-related services to tribal members who need them.

The price of health care is a major and growing worry for federal, state and local governments, which must devote a rising share of their strained budgets to paying for health care. More than forty percent of the nation's health bills are now covered by government programs. Despite this, federal monies still exist.

STATE AND REGIONAL GOVERNMENT GRANTS

• •

Before you call the contact person in your state, I
suggest that you make a list of what it is you need
monies for (i.e., hospital bills, long-term care costs, loss
of income replacement). Ask yourself such questions
as, are there demonstrated financial needs on the part
of the patient or the patient's family? In this fashion,
you can address every issue leading to support and aid
in one telephone call — by being able to describe
precisely the kinds of funding for which you may be
eligible.

When you call, ask this: "What types of funding programs do you provide?" If the response does not
include a program that meets your particular needs, ask
more specific questions. If the agency you call does
not offer a program to meet your needs, someone there
may be able to direct you to an agency that does. If
the agency publishes materials describing its funding
programs, request that these be mailed to you, along
with an application. Also make sure to find out if
there is a deadline coming up, so that you will be able
to return any applications by that time.

• •

ALABAMA

**Alabama Commission
on Aging**
2853 Fairlane Drive
Montgomery, AL 36130
(205) 832-6640

Department of Health and Human Services, Region IV Office
101 Marietta Tower
Suite 1515
Atlanta, GA 30323
(404) 331-2442

Contact: Earl Forsythe

ALASKA

Alaska Department of Health and Social Services
Office on Aging
Pouch H-01C
Juneau, AK 99811
(907) 465-3253

Department of Health and Human Services, Region X Office
2201 Sixth Avenue
RX-01
Seattle, WA 98121
(206) 553-0420

Contact: Elizabeth G. Healy

• • • • • • • • • • • • • • • • • • • •

Alaska Area Native
Health Service
P.O. Box 107741
Anchorage, AK 99510
(907) 257-1153

Program: Indian Health Service — Health Management Development Program (Federal program 93.228)
Description: Funding for American Indian/Native Alaskan projects designed to provide a full range of curative, preventive and rehabilitative health services. Assistance to federally-recognized tribes and tribal organizations. Designed to increase the capability of American Indians and Native Alaskans to manage their own health programs.
Restrictions: Only federally-recognized tribes and tribal organizations may apply
$ Given: Range of $6,250 - $6.3 million per project; average award is $62,693 (national figures)
Number of Awards: Approximately 100 awards made annually nationwide
Application Information: Contact local Health Service office for standard application forms
Deadline: Submit application 90 days prior to proposed project start date
National Contacts: Kay Carpentier, grants management contact, (301) 443-5204; or B. Bowman, program contact, (301) 443-6840
Local Contact: Gerald Ivey

ARIZONA

Arizona Department of Economic Security
Division of Aging, Family and Children's Services
1717 W. Jefferson Street
Phoenix, AZ 85005
(602) 255-3596

Department of Health and Human Services, Region IX Office
Federal Office Building
50 United Nations Plaza
Room 431
San Francisco, CA 94102
(415) 556-1961

Contact: Emory Lee

• • • • • • • • • • • • • • • • • • • •

Phoenix Area Indian Health Service
3738 North 16th Street
Suite A
Phoenix, AZ 85016-5981
(602) 241-2052
Contact: Don J. Davis
and
Navajo Area Indian Health Service
P.O. Box G
Window Rock, AZ 86515
(602) 871-5811
and
Tucson Area Indian Health Service
7900 South J. Stock Road
Tucson, AZ 85746-9352
(602) 629-6600
Contact: Eleanore Robertson

Program: Indian Health Service — Health Management Development Program (Federal program 93.228)
Description: Funding for American Indian projects designed to provide a full range of curative, preventive and rehabilitative health services. Assistance to federally-recognized tribes and tribal organizations. Designed to increase the capability of American Indians to manage their own health programs.
Restrictions: Only federally-recognized tribes and tribal organizations may apply
$ Given: Range of $6,250 - $6.3 million per project; average award is $62,693 (national figures)
Number of Awards: Approximately 100 awards made annually nationwide
Application Information: Contact local Health Service office for standard application forms
Deadline: Submit application 90 days prior to proposed project start date
National Contacts: Kay Carpentier, grants management contact, (301) 443-5204; or B. Bowman, program contact, (301) 443-6840

STATE AND REGIONAL GOVERNMENT GRANTS

• • • • • • • • • • • • • • • • • • • •

ARKANSAS

Arkansas Department of Human Services
Office on Aging and Adult Services
Donaghey Building
7th and Main Streets
Little Rock, AR 72201
(501) 371-2571

Department of Health and Human Services, Region VI Office
1200 Main Tower Building
Room 1100
Dallas, TX 75202
(214) 767-3301

Contact: J.B. Keith

CALIFORNIA

California Health and Welfare Agency
Department of Aging
918 J Street
Sacramento, CA 95814
(916) 322-5290

Department of Health and Human Services, Region IX Office
Federal Office Building
50 United Nations Plaza
Room 431
San Francisco, CA 94102
(415) 556-1961

Contact: Emory Lee

• • • • • • • • • • • • • • • • • • • •

California Area Indian Health Service
2999 Fulton Avenue
Sacramento, CA 95821
(916) 978-4202

Program: Indian Health Service — Health Management Development Program (Federal program 93.228)
Description: Funding for American Indian projects designed to provide a full range of curative, preventive and rehabilitative health services. Assistance to federally-recognized tribes and tribal organizations. Designed to increase the capability of American Indians to manage their own health programs.
Restrictions: Only federally-recognized tribes and tribal organizations may apply
$ Given: Range of $6,250 - $6.3 million per project; average award is $62,693 (national figures)
Number of Awards: Approximately 100 awards made annually nationwide
Application Information: Contact local Health Service office for standard application forms
Deadline: Submit application 90 days prior to proposed project start date
National Contacts: Kay Carpentier, grants management contact, (301) 443-5204; or B. Bowman, program contact, (301) 443-6840
Local Contact: T.J. Harwood

COLORADO

Colorado Department of Social Services
Division of Services for the Aging
1575 Sherman Street
Denver, CO 80203
(303) 839-2586

Department of Health and Human Services, Region VIII Office
Federal Building
Room 1185
1961 Stout Street
Denver, CO 80294-3538
(303) 844-3372

Contact: Paul Denham

STATE AND REGIONAL GOVERNMENT GRANTS

• • • • • • • • • • • • • • • • • • • •

CONNECTICUT

Connecticut Department on Aging
80 Washington Street
Hartford, CT 06115
(203) 566-3238

Department of Health and Human Services, Region I Office
John F. Kennedy Federal Building
Room 2411
Government Center
Boston, MA 02203
(617) 565-1500

Contact: Maureen Osolnik

DELAWARE

Delaware Department of Health and Social Services
Division of Aging
Delaware State Hospital
New Castle, DE 19720
(302) 421-6791

Department of Health and Human Services, Region III Office
3535 Market Street
Room 11480
Gateway Building
Philadelphia, PA 19104
MAIL ADDRESS: P.O. Box 13716, Mail Stop No. 1, Philadelphia, PA 19101
(215) 596-6492

Contact: James Mengel

. . . .

DISTRICT OF COLUMBIA

District of Columbia Office of the Mayor
Office of Aging
1012 14th Street, NW
Washington, DC 20005
(202) 724-5622

Department of Health and Human Services, Region III Office
3535 Market Street
Room 11480
Gateway Building
Philadelphia, PA 19104
MAIL ADDRESS: P.O. Box 13716, Mail Stop No. 1, Philadelphia, PA 19101
(215) 596-6492

Contact: James Mengel

FLORIDA

Florida Department of Health and Rehabilitation Services
Program Office of Aging and Adult Services
1323 Winewood Boulevard
Tallahassee, FL 32301
(904) 488-2650

Department of Health and Human Services, Region IV Office
101 Marietta Tower
Suite 1515
Atlanta, GA 30323
(404) 331-2442

Contact: Earl Forsythe

STATE AND REGIONAL GOVERNMENT GRANTS

• • • • • • • • • • • • • • • • • • • •

GEORGIA

Georgia Department of Human Resources
Office of Aging
47 Trinity Avenue, SW
Atlanta, GA 30334
(404) 894-4440

Department of Health and Human Services, Region IV Office
101 Marietta Tower
Suite 1515
Atlanta, GA 30323
(404) 331-2442

Contact: Earl Forsythe

HAWAII

Hawaii Executive Office on Aging
1149 Bethel Street
Honolulu, HI 96813
(808) 548-2593

Department of Health and Human Services, Region IX Office
Federal Office Building
50 United Nations Plaza
Room 431
San Francisco, CA 94102
(415) 556-1961

Contact: Emory Lee

IDAHO

Idaho Office on Aging
700 W. State
Boise, ID 83720
(208) 334-3833

Department of Health and Human Services, Region X Office
2201 Sixth Avenue
RX-01
Seattle, WA 98121
(206) 553-0420

Contact: Elizabeth G. Healy

ILLINOIS

**Illinois Department
on Aging**
421 E. Capitol Avenue
Springfield, IL 62706
(217) 785-2870

Department of Health and Human Services, Region V Office
105 West Adams
23rd Floor
Chicago, IL 60603
(312) 353-5132

Contact: Hiroshi Kanno

STATE AND REGIONAL GOVERNMENT GRANTS

• • • • • • • • • • • • • • • • • • • •

INDIANA

Indiana Commission on Aging and the Aged
Graphic Arts Building
215 N. Senate Avenue
Indianapolis, IN 46202
(317) 232-1194

Department of Health and Human Services, Region V Office
105 West Adams
23rd Floor
Chicago, IL 60603
(312) 353-5132

Contact: Hiroshi Kanno

IOWA

**Iowa Commission
on Aging**
Jewett Building
415 10th Street
Des Moines, IA 50319
(515) 281-5187

Department of Health and Human Services, Region VII Office
601 East 12th Street
Room 210
Kansas City, MO 64106
(816) 426-2821

Contact: Barbara Gumminger

· · · · · · · · · · · · · · · · · · · ·

KANSAS

**Kansas Department
of Aging**
610 W. 10th Street
Topeka, KS 66612
(913) 296-4986

Department of Health and Human Services, Region VII Office
601 East 12th Street
Room 210
Kansas City, MO 64106
(816) 426-2821

Contact: Barbara Gumminger

KENTUCKY

Kentucky Department of Human Resources
Bureau for Social Services
Office of Aging Services
Human Resources Building
275 E. Main Street
Frankfort, KY 40601
(502) 564-6930

Department of Health and Human Services, Region IV Office
101 Marietta Tower
Suite 1515
Atlanta, GA 30323
(404) 331-2442

Contact: Earl Forsythe

. . . .

LOUISIANA

Louisiana Office of Human Development
Aging Section
P.O. Box 44367
Capitol Station
Baton Rouge, LA 70804
(504) 342-2297

Department of Health and Human Services, Region VI Office
1200 Main Tower Building
Room 1100
Dallas, TX 75202
(214) 767-3301

Contact: J.B. Keith

MAINE

Maine Department of Human Services
Bureau of Maine's Elderly
State House
Augusta, ME 04333
(207) 289-2561

Department of Health and Human Services, Region I Office
John F. Kennedy Federal Building
Room 2411
Government Center
Boston, MA 02203
(617) 565-1500

Contact: Maureen Osolnik

. . . .

MARYLAND

Maryland Office on Aging
State Office Building
301 W. Preston Street
Baltimore, MD 21201
(301) 383-6393

Maryland State
Department of Health and Mental Hygiene
Services to the Aging
201 W. Preston Street
Baltimore, MD 21201
(301) 383-2723

Department of Health and Human Services, Region III Office
3535 Market Street
Room 11480
Gateway Building
Philadelphia, PA 19104
MAIL ADDRESS: P.O. Box 13716, Mail Stop No. 1, Philadelphia, PA 19101
(215) 596-6492

Contact: James Mengel

MASSACHUSETTS

Massachusetts Department of Elder Affairs
110 Tremont Street
Boston, MA 02108
(617) 727-7750

Department of Health and Human Services, Region I Office
John F. Kennedy Federal Building
Room 2411
Government Center
Boston, MA 02203
(617) 565-1500

Contact: Maureen Osolnik

STATE AND REGIONAL GOVERNMENT GRANTS

• •

MICHIGAN

Michigan Department of Management and Budget
Office of Services to the Aging
300 E. Michigan
Lansing, MI 48909
(517) 373-8230

Department of Health and Human Services, Region V Office
105 West Adams
23rd Floor
Chicago, IL 60603
(312) 353-5132

Contact: Hiroshi Kanno

MINNESOTA

Minnesota State Department of Public Welfare
Aging Program Division
658 Cedar Street
St. Paul, MN 55155
(612) 296-6193

Department of Health and Human Services, Region V Office
105 West Adams
23rd Floor
Chicago, IL 60603
(312) 353-5132

Contact: Hiroshi Kanno

• • • • • • • • • • • • • • • • • • •

Bemidji Area Indian Health Service
203 Federal Building
Bemidji, MN 56601
(218) 751-7701

Program: Indian Health Service — Health Management Development Program (Federal program 93.228)
Description: Funding for American Indian projects designed to provide a full range of curative, preventive and rehabilitative health services. Assistance to federally-recognized tribes and tribal organizations. Designed to increase the capability of American Indians to manage their own health programs.
Restrictions: Only federally-recognized tribes and tribal organizations may apply
$ Given: Range of $6,250 - $6.3 million per project; average award is $62,693 (national figures)
Number of Awards: Approximately 100 awards made annually nationwide
Application Information: Contact local Health Service office for standard application forms
Deadline: Submit application 90 days prior to proposed project start date
National Contacts: Kay Carpentier, grants management contact, (301) 443-5204; or B. Bowman, program contact, (301) 443-6840
Local Contact: Dr. Kathleen Annette, Director

MISSISSIPPI

**Mississippi Council
on Aging**
802 N. State
Jackson, MS 39201
(601) 354-6590

Department of Health and Human Services, Region IV Office
101 Marietta Tower
Suite 1515
Atlanta, GA 30323
(404) 331-2442

Contact: Earl Forsythe

. . . .

MISSOURI

Missouri Department of Social Services
Division of Aging
Broadway State Office Building
Jefferson City, MO 65102
(314) 751-3082

Department of Health and Human Services, Region VII Office
601 East 12th Street
Room 210
Kansas City, MO 64106
(816) 426-2821

Contact: Barbara Gumminger

MONTANA

Montana Department of Social and Rehabilitation Services
Aging Services Bureau
P.O. Box 4210
Helena, MT 59601
(406) 449-5650

Department of Health and Human Services, Region VIII Office
Federal Building
Room 1185
1961 Stout Street
Denver, CO 80294-3538
(303) 844-3372

Contact: Paul Denham

• • • • • • • • • • • • • • • • • • • •

Billings Area Indian Health Service
711 Central Avenue
PO Box 2143
Billings, MT 59103
(406) 657-6403

Program: Indian Health Service — Health Management Development Program (Federal program 93.228)
Description: Funding for American Indian projects designed to provide a full range of curative, preventive and rehabilitative health services. Assistance to federally-recognized tribes and tribal organizations. Designed to increase the capability of American Indians to manage their own health programs.
Restrictions: Only federally-recognized tribes and tribal organizations may apply
$ Given: Range of $6,250 - $6.3 million per project; average award is $62,693 (national figures)
Number of Awards: Approximately 100 awards made annually nationwide
Application Information: Contact local Health Service office for standard application forms
Deadline: Submit application 90 days prior to proposed project start date
National Contacts: Kay Carpentier, grants management contact, (301) 443-5204; or B. Bowman, program contact, (301) 443-6840
Local Contact: Duane L. Jeanotte

NEBRASKA

**Nebraska Commission
on Aging**
State House Station 95044
Lincoln, NE 68509
(402) 471-2306

Department of Health and Human Services, Region VII Office
601 East 12th Street
Room 210
Kansas City, MO 64106
(816) 426-2821

Contact: Barbara Gumminger

STATE AND REGIONAL GOVERNMENT GRANTS

. . . .

NEVADA

Nevada Department of Human Resources
Division for Aging Services
505 E. King Street
Carson City, NV 89710
(702) 885-4210

Department of Health and Human Services, Region IX Office
Federal Office Building
50 United Nations Plaza
Room 431
San Francisco, CA 94102
(415) 556-1961

Contact: Emory Lee

NEW HAMPSHIRE

New Hampshire State Council on Aging
14 Depot Street
Concord, NH 03301
(603) 271-2751

Department of Health and Human Services, Region I Office
John F. Kennedy Federal Building
Room 2411
Government Center
Boston, MA 02203
(617) 565-1500

Contact: Maureen Osolnik

• •

NEW JERSEY

New Jersey Department of Community Affairs
Division on Aging
363 W. State Street
Trenton, NJ 08625
(609) 292-4833

Department of Health and Human Services, Region II Office
26 Federal Plaza
Room 3835
New York, NY 10278
(212) 264-4600

Contact: Kathleen Harten

NEW MEXICO

New Mexico State Agency on Aging
Chamisa Hill Building
440 St. Michael's Drive
Santa Fe, NM 87503
(505) 827-2802

Department of Health and Human Services, Region VI Office
1200 Main Tower Building
Room 1100
Dallas, TX 75202
(214) 767-3301

Contact: J.B. Keith

. . . .

Albuquerque Area Indian Health Service
Headquarters West Indian Health Service
Federal Office Building and U.S. Courthouse
505 Marquette Avenue, NW
Suite 1502
Albuquerque, NM 87102-2162
(505) 766-2151

Program: Indian Health Service — Health Management Development Program (Federal program 93.228)
Description: Funding for American Indian projects designed to provide a full range of curative, preventive and rehabilitative health services. Assistance to federally-recognized tribes and tribal organizations. Designed to increase the capability of American Indians to manage their own health programs.
Restrictions: Only federally-recognized tribes and tribal organizations may apply
$ Given: Range of $6,250 - $6.3 million per project; average award is $62,693 (national figures)
Number of Awards: Approximately 100 awards made annually nationwide
Application Information: Contact local Health Service office for standard application forms
Deadline: Submit application 90 days prior to proposed project start date
National Contacts: Kay Carpentier, grants management contact, (301) 443-5204; or B. Bowman, program contact, (301) 443-6840
Local Contact: Eleanore Robertson

NEW YORK

New York State Office for the Aging
Agency Building 2
Empire State Plaza
Albany, NY 12223
(518) 474-4425

Department of Health and Human Services, Region II Office
26 Federal Plaza
Room 3835
New York, NY 10278
(212) 264-4600

Contact: Kathleen Harten

. . . .

NORTH CAROLINA

North Carolina Department of Human Resources
Division of Aging
325 N. Salisbury Street
Raleigh, NC 27611
(919) 733-3983

Department of Health and Human Services, Region IV Office
101 Marietta Tower
Suite 1515
Atlanta, GA 30323
(404) 331-2442

Contact: Earl Forsythe

NORTH DAKOTA

Social Service Board of North Dakota
Aging Services
State Capitol Building
Bismarck, ND 58505
(701) 224-2577

Department of Health and Human Services, Region VIII Office
Federal Building
Room 1185
1961 Stout Street
Denver, CO 80294-3538
(303) 844-3372

Contact: Paul Denham

STATE AND REGIONAL GOVERNMENT GRANTS

· ·

OHIO

Ohio Commission on Aging
50 W. Broad Street
Columbus, OH 43215
(614) 466-5500

Department of Health and Human Services, Region V Office
105 West Adams
23rd Floor
Chicago, IL 60603
(312) 353-5132

Contact: Hiroshi Kanno

OKLAHOMA

Oklahoma Department of Human Services
Special Unit on Aging
P.O. Box 25352
Oklahoma City, OK 73125
(405) 521-3531

Department of Health and Human Services, Region VI Office
1200 Main Tower Building
Room 1100
Dallas, TX 75202
(214) 767-3301

Contact: J.B. Keith

• • • • • • • • • • • • • • • • • • • •

Oklahoma City Area Indian Health Service
215 Dean A. McGee Street, NW
Oklahoma City, OK 73102-3477
(405) 237-4796

Program: Indian Health Service — Health Management Development Program (Federal program 93.228)
Description: Funding for American Indian projects designed to provide a full range of curative, preventive and rehabilitative health services. Assistance to federally-recognized tribes and tribal organizations. Designed to increase the capability of American Indians to manage their own health programs.
Restrictions: Only federally-recognized tribes and tribal organizations may apply
$ Given: Range of $6,250 - $6.3 million per project; average award is $62,693 (national figures)
Number of Awards: Approximately 100 awards made annually nationwide
Application Information: Contact local Health Service office for standard application forms
Deadline: Submit application 90 days prior to proposed project start date
National Contacts: Kay Carpentier, grants management contact, (301) 443-5204; or B. Bowman, program contact, (301) 443-6840
Local Contact: Dr. Robert Harry, Director

OREGON

Oregon Human Resources Department
Office of Elderly Affairs
772 Commercial Street, SE
Salem, OR 97310
(503) 378-4728

Department of Health and Human Services, Region X Office
2201 Sixth Avenue
RX-01
Seattle, WA 98121
(206) 553-0420

Contact: Elizabeth G. Healy

. . . .

Portland Area Indian Health Service
1220 S.W. Third Avenue
Room 476
Portland, OR 97204-2892
(503) 221-2020

Program: Indian Health Service — Health Management Development Program (Federal program 93.228)
Description: Funding for American Indian projects designed to provide a full range of curative, preventive and rehabilitative health services. Assistance to federally-recognized tribes and tribal organizations. Designed to increase the capability of American Indians to manage their own health programs.
Restrictions: Only federally-recognized tribes and tribal organizations may apply
$ Given: Range of $6,250 - $6.3 million per project; average award is $62,693 (national figures)
Number of Awards: Approximately 100 awards made annually nationwide
Application Information: Contact local Health Service office for standard application forms
Deadline: Submit application 90 days prior to proposed project start date
National Contacts: Kay Carpentier, grants management contact, (301) 443-5204; or B. Bowman, program contact, (301) 443-6840
Local Contact: Dr. Terrance Batliner, Director

PENNSYLVANIA

Pennsylvania Department of Aging
Finance Building
Room 404
Harrisburg, PA 17120
(717) 783-1550

Department of Health and Human Services, Region III Office
3535 Market Street
Room 11480
Gateway Building
Philadelphia, PA 19104
MAIL ADDRESS: P.O. Box 13716, Mail Stop No. 1, Philadelphia, PA 19101
(215) 596-6492

Contact: James Mengel

RHODE ISLAND

Rhode Island Department of Elderly Affairs
79 Washington Street
Providence, RI 02903
(401) 277-2861

Department of Health and Human Services, Region I Office
John F. Kennedy Federal Building
Room 2411
Government Center
Boston, MA 02203
(617) 565-1500

Contact: Maureen Osolnik

SOUTH CAROLINA

South Carolina State Commission on Aging
915 Main Street
Columbia, SC 29201
(803) 958-2576

Department of Health and Human Services, Region IV Office
101 Marietta Tower
Suite 1515
Atlanta, GA 30323
(404) 331-2442

Contact: Earl Forsythe

STATE AND REGIONAL GOVERNMENT GRANTS

• • • • • • • • • • • • • • • • • • • •

SOUTH DAKOTA

South Dakota Department of Social Services
Office of Adult Services and Aging
Richard F. Kneip Building
Pierre, SD 57501
(605) 773-3656

Department of Health and Human Services, Region VIII Office
Federal Building
Room 1185
1961 Stout Street
Denver, CO 80294-3538
(303) 844-3372

Contact: Paul Denham

Aberdeen Area Indian Health Service
Federal Building
115 - 4th Avenue, SE
Aberdeen, SD 57401
(605) 226-7581

Program: Indian Health Service — Health Management Development Program (Federal program 93.228)
Description: Funding for American Indian projects designed to provide a full range of curative, preventive and rehabilitative health services. Assistance to federally-recognized tribes and tribal organizations. Designed to increase the capability of American Indians to manage their own health programs.
Restrictions: Only federally-recognized tribes and tribal organizations may apply
$ Given: Range of $6,250 - $6.3 million per project; average award is $62,693 (national figures)
Number of Awards: Approximately 100 awards made annually nationwide
Application Information: Contact local Health Service office for standard application forms
Deadline: Submit application 90 days prior to proposed project start date
National Contacts: Kay Carpentier, grants management contact, (301) 443-5204; or B. Bowman, program contact, (301) 443-6840
Local Contact: Terrence Sloan, MD

• • • • • • • • • • • • • • • • • • •

TENNESSEE

Tennessee State Commission on Aging
535 Church Street
Nashville, TN 37219
(615) 741-2056

Department of Health and Human Services, Region IV Office
101 Marietta Tower
Suite 1515
Atlanta, GA 30323
(404) 331-2442

Contact: Earl Forsythe

Nashville Area Indian Health Service
3310 Perimeter Hill Drive
Nashville, TN 37211
(615) 736-5104

Program: Indian Health Service — Health Management Development Program (Federal program 93.228)
Description: Funding for American Indian projects designed to provide a full range of curative, preventive and rehabilitative health services. Assistance to federally-recognized tribes and tribal organizations. Designed to increase the capability of American Indians to manage their own health programs.
Restrictions: Only federally-recognized tribes and tribal organizations may apply
$ Given: Range of $6,250 - $6.3 million per project; average award is $62,693 (national figures)
Number of Awards: Approximately 100 awards made annually nationwide
Application Information: Contact local Health Service office for standard application forms
Deadline: Submit application 90 days prior to proposed project start date
National Contacts: Kay Carpentier, grants management contact, (301) 443-5204; or B. Bowman, program contact, (301) 443-6840
Local Contact: James Meredith

STATE AND REGIONAL GOVERNMENT GRANTS

• • • • • • • • • • • • • • • • • • •

TEXAS

Texas Governor's Committee on Aging
Executive Office Building
211 E. 7th Street
Austin, TX 78711
(512) 475-2717

Department of Health and Human Services, Region VI Office
1200 Main Tower Building
Room 1100
Dallas, TX 75202
(214) 767-3301

Contact: J.B. Keith

UTAH

Utah State Department of Social Services
Division of Aging
150 W. North Temple
Salt Lake City, UT 84103
(801) 533-6422

Department of Health and Human Services, Region VIII Office
Federal Building
Room 1185
1961 Stout Street
Denver, CO 80294-3538
(303) 844-3372

Contact: Paul Denham

. . . .

VERMONT

Vermont Agency of Human Services
Office on Aging
State Office Building
Waterbury, VT 05676
(802) 241-2400

Central Vermont Council on Aging
18 S. Main Street
Barre, VT 05641
(802) 479-0531

Department of Health and Human Services, Region I Office
John F. Kennedy Federal Building
Room 2411
Government Center
Boston, MA 02203
(617) 565-1500

Contact: Maureen Osolnik

VIRGINIA

Virginia Office of Human Resources
Office on Aging
830 E. Main Street
Richmond, VA 23219
(804) 786-7894

Department of Health and Human Services, Region III Office
3535 Market Street
Room 11480
Gateway Building
Philadelphia, PA 19104
MAIL ADDRESS: P.O. Box 13716, Mail Stop No. 1, Philadelphia, PA 19101
(215) 596-6492

Contact: James Mengel

STATE AND REGIONAL GOVERNMENT GRANTS

. . . .

WASHINGTON

Washington Department of Social and Health Services
Bureau of Aging
OB44
Olympia, WA 98504
(206) 753-2502

Department of Health and Human Services, Region X Office
2201 Sixth Avenue
RX-01
Seattle, WA 98121
(206) 553-0420

Contact: Elizabeth G. Healy

WEST VIRGINIA

West Virginia Commission on Aging
State Capitol
Charleston, WV 25305
(304) 348-3317

Department of Health and Human Services, Region III Office
3535 Market Street
Room 11480
Gateway Building
Philadelphia, PA 19104
MAIL ADDRESS: P.O. Box 13716, Mail Stop No. 1, Philadelphia, PA 19101
(215) 596-6492

Contact: James Mengel

. . . .

WISCONSIN

Wisconsin Department of Health and Social Services
Bureau of Aging
One W. Wilson Street
Madison, WI 53702
(608) 266-2536

Department of Health and Human Services, Region V Office
105 West Adams
23rd Floor
Chicago, IL 60603
(312) 353-5132

Contact: Hiroshi Kanno

WYOMING

Wyoming Department of Health and Social Services
Office on Aging
Hathaway Building
Cheyenne, WY 82002
(307) 777-7986

Department of Health and Human Services, Region VIII Office
Federal Building
Room 1185
1961 Stout Street
Denver, CO 80294-3538
(303) 844-3372

Contact: Paul Denham

STATE AND REGIONAL GOVERNMENT GRANTS

· ·

PUERTO RICO

Puerto Rico Department of Social Services
Division of Geriatrics
P.O. Box 11390
Santurce, PR 00910
(809) 724-7400

Department of Health and Human Services, Region II Office
26 Federal Plaza
Room 3835
New York, NY 10278
(212) 264-4600

Contact: Kathleen Harten

VIRGIN ISLANDS

Department of Health and Human Services, Region II Office
26 Federal Plaza
Room 3835
New York, NY 10278
(212) 264-4600

Contact: Kathleen Harten

Federal Grants

• •

The following chapter includes a limited number of health-related financial assistance programs funded by the federal government. Some of these listings (Administration on Aging, Community Health Centers) are detailed descriptions of federal programs administered through the regional offices listed in the previous chapter. If one of these programs seems appropriate for your funding needs, please refer back to the previous chapter, "State and Regional Government Grants," for the address of your local agency on aging or your regional Department of Health and Human Services office.

Other listings in this chapter include Medicare programs, funding for health services in rural communities, and several programs for U.S. veterans. If you fall into one of these funding categories, this chapter may direct you to good funding possibilities.

Remember, federal grant sources are not as narrowly defined in purpose or as accessible to individuals as private sector funders. Often, however, the dollar amounts are larger and worth the trouble.

Before you call the contact person for any agency, I suggest that you make a list of what it is you need monies for (i.e., hospital bills, long-term care costs, loss of income replacement). Ask yourself such questions as, are there demonstrated financial needs on the part of the patient or the patient's family? In this fashion, you can address every issue leading to support and aid in

. . . .

one telephone call — by being able to describe precisely the kinds of funding for which you may be eligible.

When you call, ask this: "What types of funding programs do you provide?" If the response does not include a program that meets your particular needs, ask more specific questions. If the agency you call does not offer a program to meet your needs, someone there may be able to direct you to an agency that does. If the agency publishes materials describing its funding programs, request that these be mailed to you, along with an application. Also make sure to find out if there is a deadline coming up, so that you will be able to return any applications by that time.

• • • • • • • • • • • • • • • • • • •

ADMINISTRATION ON AGING (AOA)

U.S. Department of Health and Human Services
Office of Human Development Services
Administration on Aging
HHS-N Building
330 Independence Avenue, SW
Washington, DC 20201
(202) 245-0827

Program: Administration on Aging (AOA)
Description: AOA is the principal Federal organization for identifying needs, carrying out programs (provided under the Older Americans Act), and promoting coordination of Federal resources to meet the needs of older persons. Under Title III of the Older Americans Act of 1965, AOA administers formula grants to state agencies on aging — which, in turn, serve as advocates and establish comprehensive service systems on the community level. State agencies fund local agencies. AOA makes some direct grants to qualified Indian tribal organizations.
Restrictions: Only states and qualified Indian tribal organizations may apply directly to AOA for funding. Individuals should apply through state and local agencies on aging (see previous chapter).
$ Given: Varies by state
Contact: Individuals should contact their state/local agencies on aging **(see previous chapter)**

U.S. Department of Health and Human Services
Office of Human Development Services
Administration on Aging
HHS-N Building
330 Independence Avenue, SW
Washington, DC 20201
(202) 619-0011

Program: Special Programs for the Aging — Title III, Part D; In-Home Services for Frail Older Individuals (Federal program 93.641)
Description: Formula grants to state agencies for in-home services to frail individuals, including in-home supportive services for older individuals who are victims of Alzheimer's disease and related disorders with neurological and organic brain dysfunctions, and to the families of such victims.
Restrictions: State agencies apply to Federal AOA for funding. Individuals should contact state agencies on aging for details on obtaining funds/services at the local level (see previous chapter).
$ Given: Range of $2,415 - $532,060 per grant (at federal level); average grant is $100,989 (at federal level)
Contact: Acting Associate Commissioner for State and Community Programs (at national level); or state agencies on aging **(see previous chapter)**

FEDERAL GRANTS

•   •   •   •   •   •   •   •   •   •   •   •   •   •   •   •   •   •   •   •

COMMUNITY HEALTH CENTERS

**PROGRAM
HEADQUARTERS
Division Primary Care
Services**
Bureau of Health Care
Delivery and Assistance
Health Resources and
Services Administration
Public Health Service
Department of Health and
Human Services
Room 7A-55
Parklawn Building
5600 Fishers Lane
Rockville, MD 20857
(301) 443-2260
Contact: Richard Bohrer,
Director

and

**GRANTS MANAGEMENT
Bureau of Health Care
Delivery and Assistance**
Health Resources and
Services Administration
Public Health Service
Department of Health and
Human Services
12100 Parklawn Drive
Rockville, MD 20857
(301) 443-5902
Contact: Gary Houseknecht,
Grants Management Officer

Program: Community Health Centers (Federal program
93.224)
Description: Project grants to support the development
and operation of community health centers that provide
primary and supplemental health services to medically-
underserved populations. Priority on improving availability,
accessibility and organization within these communities.
Funds may be used for buying or modernizing buildings,
as well as for acquiring special purpose equipment.
Restrictions: Public and nonprofit private agencies,
institutions and organizations, plus a limited number of
State and local governments may apply
$ Given: Range of $25,000 - $4 million per award;
average award is $1.2 million (national figures)
Application Information: Forms may be obtained from
Regional Offices of the Department of Health and Human
Services **(see previous chapter)**

• • • • • • • • • • • • • • • • • • • •

MEDICARE — HOSPITAL INSURANCE

Bureau of Program Operations
Room 300
Meadows East Building
Health Care Financing
Administration
Baltimore, MD 21207
(301) 966-5874

Program: Medicare — Hospital Insurance (Federal program 93.773)

Description: Hospital insurance protection for covered services to persons age 65 or above, as well as to certain disabled persons and individuals with chronic renal disease. Benefits paid to participating and emergency hospitals, skilled nursing facilities, home health agencies, and hospice agencies to cover reasonable cost of medically necessary services.

Restrictions: Persons age 65 and over, as well as certain disabled persons and individuals with chronic renal disease, are eligible. A person reaching age 65 after 1968 may need some work credit to qualify for hospital insurance benefits.

$ Given: Based on reasonable costs of necessary services; deductibles and co-insurance payments may be required

Application Information: Call or visit your local Social Security office; persons entitled to Social Security are enrolled automatically, without application

Contact: Local Social Security office (check telephone listings); national headquarters contact, Barbara Gagel, Director, Bureau of Program Operations

FEDERAL GRANTS

• •

MEDICARE — SUPPLEMENTARY MEDICAL INSURANCE

**Bureau of Program
Operations**
Room 300
Meadows East Building
Health Care Financing
Administration
Baltimore, MD 21207
(301) 966-5874

Program: Medicare — Supplemental Medical Insurance (Federal program 93.774)

Description: Elective medical insurance coverage for persons age 65 or over, for certain disabled persons, and for individuals with chronic renal disease. Benefits paid for reasonable charges for covered medical services.

Restrictions: All persons age 65 and over, and those under 65 who are eligible for Medicare Hospital Insurance, are eligible; enrollment is voluntary

$ Given: Individual responsible for annual $100 deductible. Thereafter, Medicare pays 80% of reasonable costs for covered services. Monthly premium is assessed; current base premium is $29.90. Some states pay the monthly premium on behalf of qualifying individuals.

Application Information: Call or visit your local Social Security office. Persons entitled to Medicare Hospital Insurance may be enrolled automatically in this program. Coverage may be declined.

Deadline: General enrollment period is the first three months of each year. If coverage is declined initially, it can be accepted later with increased monthly premiums. Special enrollment periods may be available.

Contact: Local Social Security office (check telephone listings); national headquarters contact, Barbara Gagel, Director, Bureau of Program Operations

• • • • • • • • • • • • • • • • • • •

RURAL HEALTH SERVICES OUTREACH

**PROGRAM
HEADQUARTERS
Office of Rural Health
Policy**
Health Resources and
Services Administration
Public Health Service
Room 14-22
Parklawn Building
5600 Fishers Lane
Rockville, MD 20857
(301) 443-0835
Contact: Jake Culp,
Associate Administrator

and

**GRANTS MANAGEMENT
Grants Management
Branch**
Bureau of Health Care
Delivery and Assistance
Health Resources and
Services Administration
Public Health Service
12100 Parklawn Building
Rockville, MD 20857
(301) 443-5902
Contact: Gary Houseknecht,
Grants Management Officer

Program: Rural Health Services Outreach (Federal
program 93.912)
Description: Project grants to allow for provision of
medical services to rural populations that are not
receiving them. To enhance service capacity or to expand
service area; to increase the depth and scope of health
services in rural areas.
Restrictions: Not-for-profit, public or private entities
located in a non-Metropolitan Statistical Area may apply
$ Given: Range of $50,000 - $300,000 per grant; average
grant, $200,000
Number of Awards: At least 60 awards were planned for
FY91
Application Information: Program guidelines may be
obtained from Program Headquarters; write or call the
Grants Management Officer for application kit
Deadline: Contact Program Headquarters for deadline
dates

FEDERAL GRANTS

• • • • • • • • • • • • • • • • • • • •

VETERANS HOSPITALIZATION

Director, Administrative Services
Department of Veterans Affairs
Washington, DC 20420
(202) 535-7384

Program: Veterans Hospitalization (Federal program 64.009)

Description: Provides inpatient medical, surgical and neuropsychiatric care and related medical and dental services to eligible veterans.

Restrictions: Benefits available to any veteran who (1) requires treatment for a service-connected disability or disease, or (2) has a service-connected disability but is in need of treatment for a nonservice-connected condition, or (3) has been honorably discharged and meets minimum active duty requirements, or (4) receives a VA pension, or is a former POW. Benefits are also available to the spouse or child of a veteran with total, permanent disability resulting from a service-connected disability, as well as to the widow, widower or child of a veteran who died as a result of such disability, and to the surviving spouse or child of a person who died on active duty. Medicare and CHAMPUS eligibility may interfere with VA benefits. Nonservice disabled veterans with incomes above certain levels may be treated on a resource-available basis and must agree to pay applicable co-payments.

$ Given: Services provided; approximately $7.5 billion is allotted annually nationwide for services provided through this program

Application Information: Eligible persons may apply personally at a VA Medical Center, through any veterans service organization representative, or by mailing VA Form 10-10 to the nearest VA health care facility

Contact: Local VA Medical Center

• • • • • • • • • • • • • • • • • • • •

VETERANS HOSPITAL BASED HOME CARE

Assistant Chief Medical Director for Geriatrics and Extended Care
Department of Veterans Affairs
Washington, DC 20420
(202) 535-7530

Program: Veterans Hospital Based Home Care (Federal program 64.022)
Description: Provides individual medical, nursing, social, and rehabilitative services to eligible veterans in their home environment by VA hospital staff. Provided as follow-up to inpatient status at VA facility only.
Restrictions: Open to veterans requiring intermittent skilled nursing care and related medical services for a protracted period of time. Individuals must meet criteria for VA Hospitalization (Federal program 64.009). Medical determination as to need for home health services is made by a VA hospital physician.
$ Given: Services provided; approximately $30 million allotted annually for this program, nationwide
Contact: Hospital Based Home Care Program Coordinator, or local Veterans Administration

VETERANS NURSING HOME CARE

Assistant Chief Medical Director for Geriatrics and Extended Care
Department of Veterans Affairs
Washington, DC 20420
(202) 535-7179

Program: Veterans Nursing Home Care (Federal program 64.010)
Description: Services for eligible veterans who are not acutely ill and not in need of hospital care, but who require skilled nursing care, related medical services, supportive personal care, and individual adjustment services in a homelike atmosphere.
Restrictions: Veterans must require skilled nursing care and related medical services for a protracted period of time. Individuals must meet criteria for VA Hospitalization (Federal program 64.009). Medical determination as to need for nursing home care is made by a VA hospital physician.
$ Given: Nursing home care services provided; approximately $660-$840 million allotted annually nationwide for this program
Contact: VA Nursing Home Care Program Coordinator, or local Veterans Administration

FEDERAL GRANTS

• • • • • • • • • • • • • • • • • • • •

VETERANS OUTPATIENT CARE

Director, Administrative Services
Department of Veterans Affairs
Washington, DC 20420
(202) 535-7384

Program: Veterans Outpatient Care (Federal program 64.011)
Description: Provides medical and dental services, medicines, and medical supplies to eligible veterans on an outpatient basis. Includes: examination, treatment, some home health services, podiatric, optometric, dental, supportive medical services and surgical services. Readjustment counseling for Vietnam era veterans. Drugs, medicines, prosthetic appliances, transportation, and other reasonable and necessary supplies also provided.
Restrictions: Eligibility requirements are similar but not identical to those for Veterans Hospitalization (Federal program 64.009). Check with local Veterans Administration for details.
$ Given: Services and goods provided; approximately $3 - $3.5 billion is allotted annually nationwide for this program
Contact: Local VA Medical Center

• • • • • • • • • • • • • • • • • • •

VETERANS PRESCRIPTION SERVICE

Assistant Chief Medical Director for Clinical Affairs
Department of Veterans Affairs
Washington, DC 20420
(202) 233-3277

Program: Veterans Prescription Service (Federal program 64.012)

Description: Provides eligible veterans and certain dependents and survivors with prescription drugs and expendable prosthetic medical supplies from VA pharmacies upon presentation of prescription(s) from a licensed physician. Prescriptions must be as specific therapy in treatment of illness or injury suffered by veteran; dispensed by VA pharmacists directly to veterans or dispatched through the mail. Refill service available on physician's authorization. Where there are no VA pharmacies, payment for prescribed drugs is reimbursed. Co-payment may be required from veterans with prescriptions for nonservice-related conditions.

Restrictions: Benefits available to veterans in treatment for service-connected conditions or for conditions that required hospitalization and now require continued care on an outpatient basis. Other veterans may also be eligible.

Contact: Local VA Medical Center

NATIONAL INFORMATION CENTER

U.S. Department of Health and Human Services
Office of Human Development Services
Administration on Aging
National Clearinghouse on Aging
HHS-N Building
330 Independence Avenue, SW
Washington, DC 20201
(202) 245-0188

Description: The National Clearinghouse on Aging collects, analyzes and disseminates information on such topics of aging as: nutrition, housing, health, employment, supportive social services, and legislation. The clearinghouse responds to inquiries on all aspects of aging and makes referrals to other information sources when appropriate.

Index

California Health and Welfare Agency, Department of Aging, 154
Camden Home for Senior Citizens, 16
Campbell Soup Fund, 104, 128
Carolyn Foundation, 68, 97
Carter (Amon G.) Foundation, 135
Carter (Amon G.) Star Telegram Employees Fund, 51
Cartledge Charitable Foundation, Inc., 142
CENEX Foundation, 44
Central New York Community Foundation, Inc., 109
Central Vermont Council on Aging, 179
Champion McDowell Davis Charitable Foundation, 117
Chapman Foundation, 145
Charina Foundation, Inc., 109
Child Health Foundation, 54
Christian BusinessCares Foundation, 26
Christy-Houston Foundation, 133
Clapp (Anne L. and George H.) Charitable and Educational Trust, The, 128
Clark Foundation, The, 23
Clark Foundation, The, 124
Clarke (Elizabeth Church) Testamentary Trust/Fund Foundation, The, 28
Clarke (Louis G. & Elizabeth L.) Endowment Fund, 28
Clay Foundation, 145
Close Foundation, Inc., 117, 132
Coe (Marion Isabelle) Fund, 10
Cohen (Saul Z. and Amy Scheuer) Family Foundation, Inc., The, 110
Collins Medical Trust, 125
Colorado Department of Social Services, Division of Services for the Aging, 155
Columbia Foundation, The, 91
Columbus Female Benevolent Society, 26
Commonwealth Fund, The, 110
Community Foundation of Santa Clara County, 58
Community Foundation of Shreveport-Bossier, The, 89
Community Health Centers, 186
Comprecare Foundation, Inc., 66
Conn Memorial Foundation, Inc., 72
Connecticut Department on Aging, 156
Correspondents Fund, The, 52
Coshocton Foundation, 119
CPC International Corporate Giving Program, 104
Cralle Foundation, The, 88
Crane Fund, The, 52
Cranston (Robert B.)/Pitman (Theophilus T.) Fund, 32
Crestlea Foundation, Inc., 68, 70
Crocker (James) Testamentary Trust, 11
Crocker (Mary A.) Trust, The, 58
Cutter (Albert B.) Memorial Fund, 9
Cyclops Foundation, 128

D

Dade Community Foundation, 72
Dain Bosworth/IFG Foundation, 97
Dallas Cotton Exchange Trust, 33
Dana Corporation Foundation, 120
Danforth (Josiah H.) Memorial Fund, 23
Davis (H.C.) Fund, 34
Davis (James E.) Family - W.D. Charities, 73
Davis (Tine W.) Family - W.D. Charities, Inc., 73
Dayton Foundation, The, 120
de Kay Foundation, The, 11, 22, 24
Delaware Department of Health and Social Services, Division of Aging, 156

Delaware Foundation - Quigly Trust, 12
DHHS, Alabama (Region IV), 151
DHHS, Alaska (Region X), 151
DHHS, Arizona (Region IX), 152
DHHS, Arkansas (Region VI), 154
DHHS, California (Region IX), 154
DHHS, Colorado (Region VIII), 155
DHHS, Connecticut (Region I), 156
DHHS, Delaware (Region III), 156
DHHS, District of Columbia (Region III), 157
DHHS, Florida (Region IV), 157
DHHS, Georgia (Region IV), 158
DHHS, Hawaii (Region IX), 158
DHHS, Idaho (Region X), 159
DHHS, Illinois (Region V), 159
DHHS, Indiana (Region V), 160
DHHS, Iowa (Region VII), 160
DHHS, Kansas (Region VII), 161
DHHS, Kentucky (Region IV), 161
DHHS, Louisiana (Region VI), 162
DHHS, Maine (Region I), 162
DHHS, Maryland (Region III), 163
DHHS, Massachusetts (Region I), 163
DHHS, Michigan (Region V), 164
DHHS, Minnesota (Region V), 164
DHHS, Mississippi (Region IV), 165
DHHS, Missouri (Region VII), 166
DHHS, Montana (Region VIII), 166
DHHS, Nebraska (Region VII), 167
DHHS, Nevada (Region IX), 168
DHHS, New Hampshire (Region I), 168
DHHS, New Jersey (Region II), 169
DHHS, New Mexico (Region VI), 169
DHHS, New York (Region II), 170
DHHS, North Carolina (Region IV), 171
DHHS, North Dakota (Region VIII), 171
DHHS, Ohio (Region V), 172
DHHS, Oklahoma (Region VI), 172
DHHS, Oregon (Region X), 173
DHHS, Pennsylvania (Region III), 174
DHHS, Puerto Rico (Region II), 182
DHHS, Rhode Island (Region I), 175
DHHS, South Carolina (Region IV), 175
DHHS, South Dakota (Region VIII), 176
DHHS, Tennessee (Region IV), 177
DHHS, Texas (Region VI), 178
DHHS, Utah (Region VIII), 178
DHHS, Vermont (Region I), 179
DHHS, Virgin Islands (Region II), 182
DHHS, Virginia (Region III), 179
DHHS, Washington (Region X), 180
DHHS, West Virginia (Region III), 180
DHHS, Wisconsin (Region V), 181
DHHS, Wyoming (Region VIII), 181
District of Columbia Office of the Mayor, Office of Aging, 157
Dodge Jones Foundation, 135
Donaldson (Oliver S. and Jennie R.) Charitable Trust, 93
Donaldson Foundation, The, 80, 84, 86, 89, 98, 99, 146
Dover Foundation, The, 117
Dreyfus (Max and Victoria) Foundation, Inc., The, 110
Dumke (Dr. Ezekial R. and Edna Wattis) Foundation, The, 80, 140

E

Eastman (Alexandra) Foundation, 103

W

COMPANIES/CORPORATIONS

Books in Laurie Blum's **Free Money** Series

. . . .

THE FREE MONEY FOR CHILD CARE SERIES

Free Money for Day Care
- Advice on finding financial aid for family day care, child care centers, in-house care, and camp and summer programs

Free Money for Private Schools
- Where to find money for preschool and nursery education, private primary schools, and private secondary schools

Free Money for Children's Medical and Dental Care
- Ways to receive money for both long- and short-term medical care, dental and orthodontic treatment, and dermatological procedures

Free Money for Behavioral and Genetic Childhood Disorders
- Free Money for treatment of learning disabilities, eating disorders, retardation, alcohol and drug abuse, neurological disturbances, and sleep disorders

THE FREE MONEY FOR HEALTH CARE SERIES

Free Money for Diseases of Aging
- Find money to help pay for major surgery and medical care for diseases of aging such as Alzheimer's, Parkinson's, stroke, and other chronic illnesses

Free Money for Heart Disease and Cancer Care
- Ways to receive money for the diagnosis and treatment (surgery or long-term care) of cancer and heart disease

Free Money for Fertility Treatments
- Where to look for Free Money for infertility testing, treatment, insemination, and preliminary adoption expenses

Free Money for the Care and Treatment of Mental and Emotional Disorders
- Detailed guidance on locating Free Money for psychological care